1971

The Dawn of
African History

The Dawn of
African History

EDITED BY
ROLAND OLIVER

SECOND EDITION

1968
OXFORD UNIVERSITY PRESS
NEW YORK AND LONDON

Library of Congress Catalogue Card Number: 76-78936

Maps drawn by
EDGAR HOLLOWAY

First published 1961

Second edition 1968

Printed in the United States of America

Foreword

THE HISTORY of Africa is a neglected subject, not only because the evidence for it is thin, but also because such a
variety of skills is necessary to master what evidence there is.
The written sources of African history are in English, French,
Arabic, Portuguese, Dutch, German, Italian, Afrikaans,
Amharic, Greek, Latin and Ancient Egyptian, to name only
the most important. The unwritten lore of pre-colonial times
has to be recovered from peoples speaking some six or seven
hundred other languages. The archaeological approach,
beginning with man's origins and before, and continuing right
up to the eve of the colonial period, requires as many skills as
the historical. In such a situation co-operative work is almost
essential, both in research and presentation.

This little book is an attempt at co-operative presentation.
All but three of its chapters were originally composed as part
of a series of talks broadcast by the General Overseas Service
of the B.B.C. during the summer of 1958. All the authors are
people who have made an original contribution to some aspect
of African History. Most of them know some part of Africa
intimately. A book by many hands is bound to have many
faults of construction. Yet it is hoped that these essays will at
least convey some sense of the shape of the subject as a whole,
of the lines along which work is proceeding, and, above all, of
the many problems which still need much more investigation.

Revisions have been made for the second edition to take into
account recent historical research.

Contents

FOREWORD *page iii*

1 FIRST LIGHT *Sir Mortimer Wheeler*
page 1

2 THE VALLEY OF THE NILE *A. J. Arkell*
page 7

3 CARTHAGE, GREECE AND ROME *A. A. Kwapong*
page 13

4 THE KINGDOM OF AXUM *G. W. B. Huntingford*
page 22

5 THE INVADING CRESCENT *Bernard Lewis*
page 30

6 KINGDOMS OF THE WESTERN SUDAN *Thomas Hodgkin*
page 37

7 THE LAND OF ZANJ *Gervase Mathew*
page 45

8 THE RIDDLE OF ZIMBABWE *Roland Oliver*
page 53

9 PEOPLES AND KINGDOMS OF THE CENTRAL SUDAN
D. H. Jones
page 60

10 STATES OF THE GUINEA FOREST *J. D. Fage*
page 68

11 THE OLD KINGDOM OF CONGO *C. R. Boxer*
page 75

12 SOUTH OF THE CONGO *J. Vansina*
page 82

13 SOUTH OF THE LIMPOPO *W. M. Macmillan*
page 88

14 THE AFRICAN ACHIEVEMENT *Roland Oliver*
page 96

INDEX
page 104

List of Maps

1 *North East Africa, showing the main trade routes*   *page* 8

2 *Greek and Roman North Africa*   14

3 *The Sphere of Axum*   24

4 *Islam in North Africa*   32

5 *The Kingdoms of the Western Sudan*   38

6 *Medieval East Africa*   46

7 *Trade Routes of the Indian Ocean in the Fifteenth Century*   49

8 *Medieval Rhodesia*   54

9 *Peoples and Kingdoms of the Central Sudan*   62

10 *States of the Guinea Forest*   69

11 *The Kingdom of Congo and its Neighbours*   76

12 *Peoples of West Central Africa*   83

13 *South of the Limpopo*   89

List of Plates

1. ZINJANTHROPUS : NUTCRACKER MAN
(*Photograph: Dr. L. S. B. Leakey*)

2A. THE PYRAMIDS AT MEROE
(*Photograph: Basil Davidson*)

2B. SABRATHA: THE FORUM AS SEEN LOOKING NORTH-
WEST OVER THE ADJACENT RUINS
(*Photograph: Mrs. A. C. Cook*)

3. OBELISK AT AXUM
(*Photograph: M. Albert Guillot*)

4. KAYRAWĀN : MINARET OF GREAT MOSQUE
(*Photograph: Professor K. A. Cresswell*)

5A. MOSQUE OF SANKORLÉ : MINARET AND TOWER OF THE
MIHRAB
(*Photograph: R. Mauny, I.F.A.N.*)

5B. NABHANI MOSQUE ON SOŊGO MNARA : MIHRAB LATE
FOURTEENTH TO EARLY FIFTEENTH CENTURY
(*Photograph: Tanganyika Public Relations Office*)

6. BATTLE OF AMBUILA, 1665, AS DEPICTED IN GLAZED TILES
OF ONE SEVENTEENTH CENTURY HERMITAGE OF NAZARÉ,
LUANDA
(*Photograph: Professor C. R. Boxer*)

7. ZIMBABWE : VIEW FROM THE ACROPOLIS
(*Photograph: Caroline Oliver*)

8. IFE BRONZEWORK : A KING AND A QUEEN
(*Photograph: Federal Ministry of Information, Nigeria*)

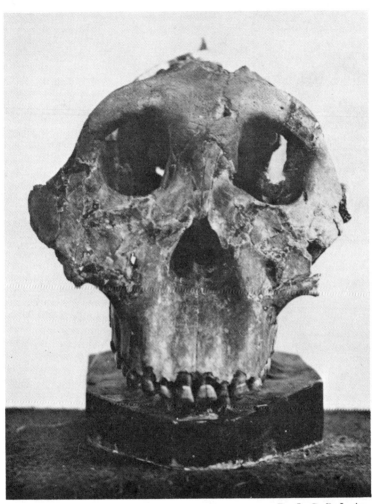

Dr. L. S. B. Leakey

1. ZINJANTHROPUS: NUTCRACKER MAN

Basil Davidson

2A. THE PYRAMIDS AT MEROF

Mrs. A. C. Cook

2B. SABRATHA: THE FORUM AS SEEN LOOKING NORTH-WEST
OVER THE ADJACENT RUINS

M. *Albert Guillot*

3. OBELISK AT AXUM

Professor K. A. Cresswell

4. KAYRAWĀN: MINARET OF GREAT MOSQUE

R. Mauny: I. F. A. N.

5A. MOSQUE OF SANKORÉ:
MINARET AND TOWER OF THE MIHRAB

Tanganyika Public Relations Office

5B. NABHANI MOSQUE ON SONGO MNARA:
MIHRAB LATE FOURTEENTH TO EARLY FIFTEENTH CENTURY

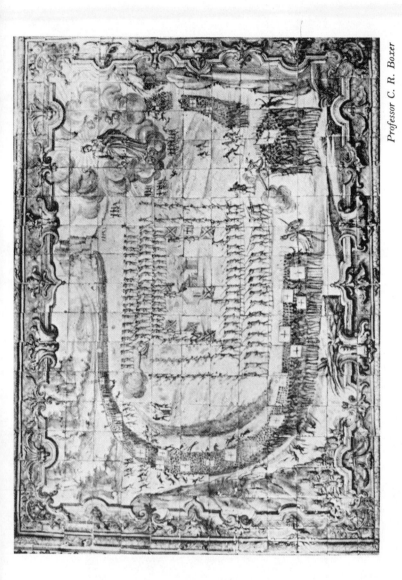

6. BATTLE OF AMBUILA, 1665, AS DEPICTED IN GLAZED TILES OF ONE SEVENTEENTH
CENTURY HERMITAGE OF NAZARÉ, LUANDA

7. ZIMBABWE: VIEW FROM THE ACROPOLIS

Federal Ministry of Information, Nigeria

8. IFE BRONZEWORK: A KING AND A QUEEN

The Dawn of
African History

CHAPTER ONE

First Light

Sir Mortimer Wheeler

ASIA IS the undisputed homeland of civilization: Africa may well be the homeland of man himself. I find that thought a salutary corrective when, as an archaeologist who has worked in Asia, I compare the one continent with the other. In this sort of comparison one tends to group ancient Egypt with Asia; but even if we include Egypt, as racially and geographically we should, in Africa, my opening remark holds good. The civilization of Dynastic Egypt is nowadays admitted to be secondary to that of Mesopotamia. Asia leads the way in human progress; but it is by no means certain that the Garden of Eden, or its more scientific equivalent, should not be located in Africa.

That is one of the things which make research into Africa's past so difficult. Civilized man has many ways of self-expression. Even if his literature is inadequate or non-existent, his houses and towns and public buildings, his crafts and the products of his trafficking, his art and his household-goods, all help us to rediscover the sort of man he was and something of his relations with the outside world. In a large part of Africa these aids are lacking. In spite of skilled and persistent investigations during the last few decades, our present ignorance of pre-European Africa is abysmal. It is little more advanced than was our knowledge of African geography before the generation of Livingstone got to work upon it. Even of the Negro, whose part in world affairs grows apace, we know astonishingly little; where he came from, when, and how.

In glancing at our present knowledge of these and other matters, we may here write off two regions of Africa which

1

have long looked outwards to worlds across the seas. The first of these is the Mediterranean coastland which has always been inclined to share its ideas with Europe. The second is the East African coastline, the coastline of what we know as Somalia, Kenya, and Tanzania, which has long shared its life with Arabia and India and continues to do so today. But apart from those two peripheral zones, and apart of course from the receding domination of European colonists elsewhere, Africa belongs to itself, even when, as in South Africa, its present problems have a European background.

I have said that Africa may well be the homeland of man himself. The physical ancestry of man is a difficult problem, full of pitfalls and uncertainties. It is easy even for experts, who are on the lookout for traps, to mistake ancestral man's apish cousins for his true parents, and so to get the human family tree all wrong. Nevertheless there are some scientists who would see in certain half-man, half-ape skeletons from the Transvaal, and more recently from Tanzania, likely candidates for the status of proto-man.

The Transvaal type is known as *Australopithecus*, and may have lived a million or more years ago. He had a projecting face, more or less human teeth, and a brain more developed than that of any of the existing apes. Moreover, there is a suspicion that this early South African, unlike the apes, could already make and use tools or weapons of a primitive kind: bone clubs and roughly chipped pebbles. He certainly appears to have walked upright, thus releasing his hands for all manner of mischief. It may be that he was the first sub-human troublemaker; the preliminary sketch of a human being.

The Tanzania skull, nicknamed 'Nutcracker Man' by Dr. L. S. B. Leakey who found it at Olduvai in 1959, is related to *Australopithecus*. Around it were rough stone artifacts, of which the creature was at first thought to have been the author. Subsequently, at a slightly lower level in the same geological formation, remains of a somewhat more 'advanced' hominid were brought to light and christened *Homo habilis;* and there is now an inclination to regard *him* as the authentic tool-maker. Two tests applied to the environing volcanic rock have given a consistent antiquity: roughly, 1¾ million years by the potassium-argon method, and 2 million years, plus or minus half-a-million, by uranium fission-track tests.

These new dates have carried the antiquity of mankind appreciably further back than had previously been accepted as a scientific convention. But the revolution has not stopped there. More recently, Dr. Leakey has re-examined the whole problem of the age of separation of the family of man from that of the apes. In 1961 remains of a primate which has been named *Kenyapithecus wickeri* were found at Fort Ternan in Kenya and, combined with a reappraisal of a former discovery in the Siwaliks of Pakistan, suggested the existence of proto-men in Africa and the Indian subcontinent something like 12 million years ago. Spurred on by this discovery, Dr. Leakey undertook the re-assessment of early Miocene fossils found in Kenya and Uganda since 1931, and regards them as hominid; the rocks which covered them have been dated by the potassium-argon technique to more than 19.8 million years ago. There for the moment the matter rests; it would appear that there were in East Africa creatures within the range of human variation something like 20 million years ago.

Whatever be the ultimate scientific judgement on these remote creatures, there is at least no doubt that a number of later but still very ancient Africans, known to us by their distinctive bones and artifacts, fall within the human orbit. Half a million years ago and less, a large and diversified proto-human population roamed about the continent in perpetual search of food. This population armed itself with a variety of clubs and stone weapons, of which the latter are increasingly familiar to research. For example, at Olorgesaile, about forty miles from Nairobi, vast numbers—several thousands—of so-called hand-axes of chipped stone are still lying about where they have been lying this two or three hundred thousand years. With these large pear-shaped implements, men or sub-men dug edible roots, and slew and skinned animals, and broke bones for marrow. Clumsy instruments, perhaps, these 'hand-axes', but at one time the most widely distributed type of implement in the world. They occur all over Africa, except in the central forest zone; I have picked them up in peninsular India; many thousands have been recovered from the gravels of Middlesex. Within that vast expanse of the earth's surface, ranging from England to India, Africa is the central and most productive region. It is difficult not to suppose that Africa led the way in this ancient and far-flung technique.

Indeed, throughout that immense period which we know as the Old Stone Age, Africa seems, intermittently at least, to have been in the lead. Subsequently, beginning perhaps ten or a dozen thousand years ago, western Asia usurped the leadership. The herd-animals and crop-plants which were destined to form the main basis of modern food-production occurred in the wild state between the eastern Mediterranean and Iran or north-west India. It was therefore in that part of the world, western Asia, that the greatest social revolution in the whole story of man occurred; the great change-over from the restless anxieties of food-gathering to the comparatively settled certainties of farming. That revolution made civilization possible; hence civilization also is an Asian product. Five or six thousand years ago it extended to the Nile Valley, and at various times stock-farming and rudimentary agriculture have penetrated further in Africa; but until quite recent times the African remained a hunter and food-collector rather than a food-producer. In sociological terms he remained a savage or, at best, a barbarian in a rich natural environment, lacking the stimulus required to turn him into a citizen.

I have just spoken of 'the' African, but of course, like Charles Dickens's Mrs. Harris, 'there's no sich person'. European and Asian settlers apart, Africa is an amalgam of races and languages which have been as inextricably confused by scholarship as by nature. In excuse, we may recall that our first acquaintance with Africa south of the Sahara is no older than the fifteenth century; that the Cape was first rounded by a European in 1487; and that the source of the Nile was not discovered until 1863. Our records are therefore absurdly recent.

Today it is often broadly asserted that there are five main groups of Africans. First there are the so-called 'aboriginal' Bushmen of the Kalahari region, Hottentots of the south-west, and Pygmies of the Congo forests. (The word 'aboriginal' is merely a term which masks our ignorance.) Secondly, there are the so-called 'true Negroes' of West Africa. Thirdly, there are the so-called 'Bantu Negroes' who occupy most of Africa south of the equator. But 'Bantu' is not really a race term but a language term, and the phrase 'Bantu Negroes' is therefore an unscientific one. Fourthly, there are the diverse 'Hamitic Negroes' of north-eastern and east-central Africa. The Hamites have mixed with the Negroes but are themselves not Negroes at all; the pre-Dynastic Egyptians were Hamites, as are many of the Saharan nomads and the berbers of the Barbary coast. Therefore, fifthly, there are the non-Negroid inhabitants of North Africa, including Hamites and Arabs.

The biggest and most interesting problem remains that of the Negroes themselves. The origin of the Negro has been sought in southern Europe, in India, in south-western Asia. Daring speculators have even suggested that the Negro may have originated in Africa itself. It is recognized that throughout southern Asia—in parts of India, Melanesia, and Australia—are groups of people showing negroid characteristics. The two famous Grimaldi skulls of the Old Stone Age, perhaps 200,000 years ago, found in the south of France and now preserved at Monaco, also have negroid traits but were not, in the skeletal sense, true Negroes.

Indeed, it is a remarkable fact that, among a growing accumulation of ancient human skulls from Africa and the adjacent continents, there is no clear Negro prototype. The fact is that we simply do not know the racial history of the

Negro. In Africa there has been a tendency, in relatively recent times, for him to work his way southwards; and it is
only fair to note that he had not yet reached the southernmost
tip of the continent when the first European settlements
were made at the Cape. But, generally speaking, what has
been called 'the Negro enigma' persists: a proper subject
for continued study in the light, it is to be hoped, of fresh
discovery.

This brief survey would be incomplete and indeed unfair if
it did not refer to two outstanding achievements of West
Africa in the field of art and craftsmanship. Negro craftsmanship as a whole rarely rises above the level of what may be
called, a little patronizingly, 'folk art'. But Nigeria has produced two notable groups of sculptures far above the folk-art
level. In 1938, in the middle of the town of Ife, an astonishing
collection of brass heads was unearthed, and drew the world's
attention to a school of art of which only too little is as yet
known. The heads are skilfully cast—they are portraits,
presumably royal portraits—and are vivid and masterly
representations, with a combined restraint and naturalism
that remind one in skill of the best portraiture of Dynastic
Egypt. Where the sculptors learned their craft is equally a
mystery. Even their date, beyond the probability that it is
before rather than after the fifteenth century, is mere con-
jecture.

The other group is also from Nigeria and is well known;
it is the famous collection of bronze (or brass) and ivory
craftsmanship from Benin, found there in 1897. Some of this
Benin art represents Western traders in their sixteenth- and
seventeenth-century costumes. A few of the Benin bronzes
are reminiscent of the Ife heads, though they never attain to
the same standard of artistry. But Ife and Benin between them
show that at the end of our Middle Ages, if not before,
African art at its best had reached a very high level indeed.
Genius may flourish in a grass hut as it has flourished traditionally in a garret. Who knows what developing African
research may yet reveal?

CHAPTER TWO

The Valley of the Nile

A. J. Arkell

As you go from north to south, Africa consists of a series of belts of very different country running from east to west across the continent. South of the fertile Mediterranean belt, where winter rains fall, is a deep belt which includes the Libyan Desert and the Sahara, in the middle of which is one of the hottest and driest deserts in the world, although there are in it a few widely separated oases caused by the wind hollowing out the sandstone (where it is soft enough) right down to the water table. To the south of the desert is a belt of country where the summer rains produce vegetation which gradually thickens from grass to sparse bush, and so to thick bush and then to tropical forest around the equator. The middle of this belt of vegetation, the Sudan belt, is the richest economically, and provides the easiest route for people travelling across the continent from east to west or vice versa, because there water holes are not too far apart and the bush is not too thick.

During the five thousand years or so since history began in ancient Egypt, the desert belt has been gradually expanding, with the result that what was the best east to west route 5,000 years ago is now to all intents desert; while the best route now was then in the impenetrable forest. Across these belts of varying country, the Nile, which rises in the mountainous country near the Equator, cuts at right angles, and thus forms a connecting link across the desert between the coastal region and the land of Egypt on the one hand and the fertile central Sudan. From the moment that history begins in Egypt about 3000 B.C., when a conqueror, perhaps of Asian

7

origin, united Upper Egypt to the land of the Delta, and set up the kingdom that was to last with various ups and downs for nearly three thousand years, this kingdom began at once to spread its influence southwards into Africa. By 2700 B.C. the king had become regarded as divine, as responsible for the fertility of the country, and as the representative on earth of a god, whom at death he rejoined in the sky. Near Wadi Halfa, at the natural frontier made by the second cataract of

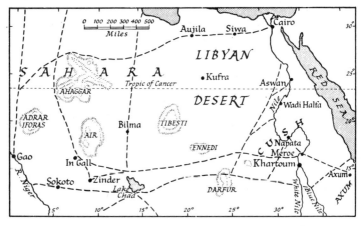

1. North East Africa, showing the main trade routes

the Nile, there is a picture engraved on a rock recording the conquest of that area by a king of the First Dynasty of Egypt, showing the local chief a prisoner and the corpses of his followers floating in the river. Some five or six centuries later, Egyptian merchant adventurers inscribed on their tombs at Aswan accounts of how they explored overland south and west of the first cataract with donkey caravans, probably reaching the Lake Chad region or even northern Nigeria, bringing back African commodities, such as frankincense, ebony, leopard-skins, ivory, and, in one case, a dancing dwarf. Other traders may have found their way by a more northerly route from oasis to oasis as far as the Niger.

By 2000 B.C. a series of massive mud-brick forts had been built on the Nile to hold the frontier between Egypt and its southern neighbour, Cush, and to protect the frontier town which had grown up near Wadi Halfa: while ahead of the frontier a trading centre was set up at the headquarters of the prince of Cush. Stone copies of the two-lugged copper axe so characteristic of Egypt at this period have been found not only there but in several places across country to the west as far as Nigeria itself, showing that at least one influence from Egypt found its way to West Africa at that time.

This region in the Valley of the Nile, just across Egypt's southern border was in fact the vital channel through which the influence of ancient Egypt passed southwards into the rest of Africa. The Egyptians called it Cush and it was known later in the Middle Ages as Nubia. The history of Cush was closely bound up with that of Egypt, and at one period it was colonized and incorporated into Egypt itself. This happened in about 1500 B.C. Evidence of the Egyptian occupation of the land of Cush is to be found in the ruins of the fine stone temples which they built in almost every small town.

The frequent representation of Negro Africans and of monkeys in Egyptian art of this period shows clearly the contact with the land of the Negroes that Egypt was making then for the first time. Also, in my opinion, few if any of the rock paintings south of the desert are earlier than about 1500 B.C., when the decorated walls of the temples built by the Egyptians in Cush possibly first gave African peoples the idea of painting pictures. Further evidence of Egyptian influence making itself felt in Africa at this time is the survival among certain chiefs' regalia in equatorial Africa of the 'leg of mutton' knife, the *khepesh*, which was introduced to Egypt from Asia as a royal emblem about 1300 B.C.

Some five centuries after its incorporation in Egypt, the land of Cush was lost to an Egypt that had become so corrupt and so degenerate that no documents record what happened. And about 700 B.C., the tables were actually turned. The rulers of Cush made expeditions to Egypt which led to their occupation of that country as reformers whose aim was to bring Egypt back to the religion and customs it had practised a thousand or more years earlier. For two generations they restored to some extent the greatness of Egypt, and much increased the prosperity of their homeland, the northern Sudan, building great temples there in Egyptian style. It is probable that under their empire the cultural influence of Egypt extended as much as 500 miles south of Khartoum, for the Nilotics of the Upper Nile are mentioned in the book of the prophet Isaiah as 'a people tall and smooth, whose land the rivers divide'.

But at the other end of their domain, where Egypt borders on Palestine, the Cushites clashed with the expanding military nation of Assyria, whose troops were armed with plenty of weapons of the new metal, iron, against which the primitive weapons of the Cushite tribesmen were of no avail. They were driven back to the Sudan, and with Assyrian support a rival dynasty was set up in Egypt, that came from the Delta and bore much ill-feeling towards the Cushites for enslaving some of their womenfolk and sending them to serve as slaves in the temples of the Sudan. Fearing the Cushites would again invade Egypt, about 591 B.C., the pharaoh sent an expedition, of which the spearhead was formed by a body of Greek and Carian mercenaries armed with the new iron weapons. This expedition sacked the old Cushite capital of Napata and caused the move of the capital to Meroe farther south.

Here at Meroe, where both iron-stone and wood fuel were available, the Cushites about this time set about manufacturing iron weapons and tools on such a scale that, after examining the slag heaps through which the railway now runs on its way to Khartoum, one archaeologist described Meroe as having been the Birmingham of Africa. I have seen them myself and I think this is a fair description. No doubt the process of iron-smelting was kept for a long time as secret as processes connected with the fusion of the atom are today, and this probably accounts for the strange taboos and customs in connexion with iron-working that still survive in many parts of Africa. There is no reason to think that iron-smelting was invented independently in Negro Africa, but every reason to believe that the knowledge of iron-working was gradually diffused over Africa from the Cushite capital Meroe.

The royal family of Cush, after their expulsion from Egypt, continued to rule the northern Sudan for the best part of a thousand years. Their burials were at first in fine stone sarcophagi inscribed with Egyptian ritual texts in correct hieroglyphs, in chambers under well-built pyramids of stone masonry, then with no sarcophagi and less well-built stone pyramids, with inscriptions first in a local form of hiero-glyphs; then with no inscriptions at all, and finally under tiny pyramids of red brick. These customs of burial show vividly how the once flourishing Egyptian culture degenerated when it was cut off from its homeland. But the idea of the divine king and the knowledge of iron-working, both derived from Egypt, were never lost, though the knowledge of writing was.

Meroe's neighbour to the east was the kingdom of Axum. In the fourth century A.D., Axum, probably for reasons of trade rivalry, for it had risen to power on the control of eastern products in demand in the Roman world, picked on an unimportant border affray between nomads as an excuse for attacking and overthrowing a senile Meroe, in order to secure the gold which reached the Mediterranean from West Africa as well as from the head-waters of the Blue Nile on the borders of Abyssinia. And we can infer from one inscription and from ruins, and from the traditions of various divine kingdoms that stretch all the way across to the Atlantic, that after the fall of Meroe the royal family that had ruled there for more than a thousand years moved west, away from the Nile, along that easiest of all routes between the desert and the forest, and sired many another little kingdom where the ruler was divine and the institutions reflected the degenerate Egyptian institutions of Meroe. With them went the know-ledge of iron-working across Africa. On that route Lake Chad is something of a Clapham Junction, and it is probable that once iron-working was known in that area it was diffused by more than one route into Africa south as well as west of Chad.

But it is to the Nile Valley that we look for the original link between Egypt and all Africa south of it—and in the Nile Valley specially to the Cushite capital of Meroe. Meroe's name has come to stand for a significant phase in African history: a meeting point of cultures and above all a channel for the diffusion of the knowledge of making and using iron.

CHAPTER THREE

Carthage, Greece and Rome

A. A. Kwapong

NORTH AFRICA has two faces like the Roman god Janus; one looks northwards towards the Mediterranean, the other southwards towards the Sahara. Both these two elements of sea and desert have exercised a decisive influence on the rich and varied history of its peoples. The role of the Mediterranean is better known to students of classical antiquity. Modern travellers throughout North Africa are still to this day vividly reminded of the vanished world of Punic, Greek and Roman Africa by the magnificent ruins of such cities as Cyrene, Leptis Magna, Sabratha, Carthage, Timgad and Volubilis—not to mention the profusion of ancient olive-presses, fortified farms, dams and barrages in the wadis, and Roman milestones which still stand on the routes which led into the desert. The patient work of scholars and archaeologists from many countries has revealed within the past few decades many rich treasures which have lain buried—and hence been preserved—beneath the sands for many centuries, and our knowledge of the various civilizations which flourished in North Africa within the classical era has thereby been greatly enlarged. In particular, welcome light has recently been thrown on the role which the Sahara and the peoples within and south of it played in the fortunes of North Africa, and even if many of the details of the picture still remain to be filled in, the outlines are not as blurred as they used to be.

Our story begins at the turn of the first millennium B.C.—a convenient but artificial landmark. If we look at the Middle East, the scene was briefly as follows: The great river

13

valley civilizations of Egypt and Sumer had passed their prime and were entering upon a period of general decline, during which they fell a prey first to Assyria and later to Persia. In the Aegean Basin, the domination of the Hittites in Asia Minor and of Mycenae on the Greek mainland was coming to an end. The latter had supplanted the brilliant

2. *Greek and Roman North Africa*

naval empire of Minoan Crete but was itself disintegrating before the influx of the Dorians, other Greek-speaking immigrants from the north. In Syria-Palestine, the home of various Semitic peoples who had been subjected in turn by Egypt and Mesopotamia, the leading maritime states were the Phoenician cities of Tyre and Sidon. West of Egypt, the rest of North Africa was inhabited by various loosely-organized Hamitic peoples who collectively came to be known as Libyans. These were the ancestors of the modern Berbers, who were either pastoral nomads or sedentary cultivators of

14

the coastal belt of North Africa. The most fertile sections of the North African coast suitable for settlement were Cyrenaica in modern Libya, and the Maghreb, which is now Tunisia, Algeria and Morocco. But North Africa, west of Egypt, was still an unknown mystery to the northern Mediterranean peoples, although echoes of it may be detected in the *Odyssey* of Homer and the wanderings of the Argonauts. The significant end of this period of unsettlement and the upheavals of peoples was the emergence of the Phoenicians and the Greeks as the two outstanding rivals in trade and colonization throughout the whole of the Mediterranean Basin, and the expansion of these two peoples remained the dominant factor in the history of the next five centuries at the close of which both had established flourishing colonies on the northern littoral of Africa.

The Phoenicians were the first to be attracted to the western Mediterranean by the lucrative trade in the tin and silver of the biblical Tarshish in southern Spain, and by the twelfth century B.C. they had sailed beyond the Straits of Gibraltar and founded settlements at Lixus on the Atlantic coast of Morocco, and at Gades at the mouth of the Guadalquivir in Spain. The power of the Phoenicians increased from this profitable trade and soon other trading posts which they established in the islands and around the littoral of the western Mediterranean basin had been transformed into flourishing colonies. Of their colonies in Africa—or Libya, as it was known to the Greeks—Utica was the oldest and Carthage became the greatest. This city was founded in the ninth century B.C. There is no space to recall in detail the romantic legend of the city's foundation by the royal Elissa and her band of aristocratic exiles which the poet Virgil has made famous, nor to trace the stages of her rapid growth in the next three centuries until she became the mistress of a far-flung and prosperous empire. Her territorial possessions included a part of Tunisia with the neighbouring Libyan tribes as either her subjects or allies with whom the Carthaginians intermarried and from whom they recruited mercenaries for their armies. The rest of the Maghreb, southern Spain, Sardinia, Corsica and, in particular, Sicily, were all dotted with Carthaginian trading posts and colonies, and the western Mediterranean Basin was transformed into a jealously-guarded preserve from which all foreign rivals were excluded. Treaties have survived showing that even the Romans with whom they were in alliance were kept out from the Carthaginian west, but it was with the Greeks that they waged a bitter and ceaseless struggle, especially over the island of Sicily. These people, their greatest rivals, had established prosperous colonies in Cyrenaica since the seventh century B.C. and here they exploited the agricultural wealth of the region, and developed the characteristic political and cultural institutions of Greek city-states in association with the neighbouring Libyans. When they attempted, however, in the sixth century B.C. to expand westwards into present-day Tripolitania, they were similarly kept out by the Carthaginians.

Trade was the basis of the Carthaginian State, and the lucrative profit they derived from their western markets accounts for their exclusiveness. The principal commodities included textiles, purple dye, pottery, glassware, ivory, precious stones such as carbuncles which some have identified with aggrey beads, and gold. The silent barter in gold which they practised with the natives of the west coast is described in a well-known passage of Herodotus. This is what he has to say:

'The Carthaginians also tell us that they trade with a race of men who live in a part of Libya beyond the Pillars of Hercules. On reaching this country, they unload their goods, arrange them tidily along the beach, and then, retiring to their boats, raise a smoke. Seeing the smoke, the natives come down to the beach, place on the ground a certain quantity of gold in exchange for the goods, and go off again to a distance. The Carthaginians then come ashore and take a look at the gold; and if they think it represents a fair price for their wares, they collect it and go away; if, on the other hand, it seems too little, they go back aboard and wait, and the natives come and add to the gold until they are satisfied. There is perfect honesty on both sides; the Carthaginians never touch the gold until it equals in value what they have offered for sale, and the natives never touch the goods until the gold has been taken away.'

The same historian also reports the circumnavigation of Africa by Phoenician sailors on the orders of the Egyptian Pharaoh Necho in the sixth century, but the only authentic information we possess on their maritime ventures is the so-called *Periplus* of Hanno, an account of a journey along the west coast of Africa which is to be dated to the fifth century B.C. Although the limits of this expedition are still disputed by scholars, the view that Hanno reached some point on the Guinea coast seems not unreasonable. How far these intrepid traders penetrated southwards across the Sahara from their cities on the Syrtic coast remains also a mystery which has led some to discern Punic influence in West African culture and art, but this is only speculation.

The expansion of Rome in the third century into a Mediterranean power naturally brought her into collision with Carthage and led to the life-and-death struggle of the Punic Wars which produced such great names as Hamilcar Barca and Hannibal on the Carthaginian side and Scipio Africanus on the Roman. When eventually Rome destroyed Carthage in 146 B.C., and ploughed and doomed her site to a perpetual curse, it looked as if, after an existence of seven centuries, the city and her people had been completely blotted out from the face of the earth. Yet one of the most interesting features of North African history is the persistence with which Punic civilization carried on after the fall of the city and survived far into the later years of the Roman Empire. Nor is this surprising when one remembers that not all the Punic cities shared the fate of Carthage: cities like Utica which had deserted to the Roman side were spared, and from these centres, Punic life and ways continued to flourish. But the chief inheritors of this civilization were the Berber kingdoms which had been influenced through various ties of intermarriage and alliance with the Carthaginians, and which had played such a signal part in the destruction of the city. Punic libraries were presented to various African princes by the Roman Senate, and King Juba of Mauretania gained a considerable reputation for his erudition in Punic writings. St Augustine mentions a number of Carthaginian books in his time in which many wise sayings had been recorded. Punic culture, especially religious practices, made an indelible mark on the Berbers. Recent finds in Punic cemeteries have confirmed that, on the whole, this religion was of a gloomy nature and that the Carthaginians resorted to human sacrifices: the stories of the Greek and Roman writers that the Carthaginians offered their children to Moloch have been proved true by the discovery of the calcined remains of several children in a Punic shrine. If Tertullian is to be believed, this rite persisted into the first century A.D. until its suppression by the Roman emperors.

Perhaps the reputation of Carthage has been ill-served by the material remains she left behind, most of which are not impressive. The art objects which date from the truly Punic period unearthed in the cemeteries, such as lamps, medallions, sculptured heads of gods and goddesses, are for the most part Greek or Oriental importations or indifferent copies, and justify the harsh verdict of posterity on this city 'in which money was the first preoccupation and art or letters the last.' It is true however that a vigorous native tradition of art and culture in Numidia and Mauretania arose after the fall of Carthage which derived its inspiration from a fusion of Punic and Libyan elements. Examples of this art are the impressive monumental tombs, the Medcracen north of the Aures Mountains and the Tomb of the Christian west of Algiers, and masterpieces such as the funerary lions of Mactar which were produced in remote and secluded areas.

With the establishment of the Roman Empire along the whole length of the North African littoral, the country and its peoples entered into closer political, economic and cultural ties with the imperial city. The Maghreb became the granary of Rome, and Roman rule was primarily concerned with the agricultural exploitation of the cultivable coastal zone. The production of corn, olives and vines and other fruits which had been developed by the Carthaginians and taken over in their kingdoms by the Numidians was intensified, and the relics of olive-presses, fortified farms, and Roman hydraulic engineering scattered all over the length and breadth of North Africa still pay an eloquent tribute to the success of the Roman occupation. Side by side with this growing prosperity went, in the course of the first three centuries of the Christian era, the growth of urban and municipal life. This prosperity is most evident in the reign of the emperors of the Severan dynasty, who were themselves of North African descent. Most of the finest buildings in North Africa, at Leptis, Sabratha, Timgad, Volubilis in the west and in the Greco-Roman centres of the Cyrenaican Pentapolis in the east all date to this period of imperial and municipal splendour. The inscriptions and other ancient evidence show that the process of Romanization was extended to many of the indigenous village communities many of which attained the status of Roman colonies and their inhabitants Roman citizenship.

Although the writ of the Romans ran through the whole length of North Africa, they never really succeeded in extending their control into the heart of the desert. In the absence of natural barriers along the southern frontier of Roman Africa, the prosperity and expansion of the provinces were always threatened by the incursions and forays of desert marauders like the Garamantes and the Gaetuli who coveted the wealth of the coast and naturally resented the limitation to their freedom of movement and grazing rights. This became the central military problem in the Roman occupation of Africa. The Roman answer to the depredations of these restless Libyan tribes of the interior was the construction of artificial frontier defences, which consisted of fortified settlements at well-chosen points, manned by soldier-farmers, many of whom were of local descent. These *limes*, as they were called, served both as a defensive barrier and a line of demarcation between cultivated land and desert country. At various times, the

Romans had to undertake expeditions into the desert, the most famous of which were those of Cornelius Balbus in 19 B.C., and of Septimius Flaccus and Julius Maternus about half a century later. Maternus penetrated as far as Agysimba, perhaps the oasis of Asben or Tibesti, half-way across the Sahara.

These expeditions may not all have been punitive in aim: excavations by Italian archaeologists have shown that Roman trade-goods such as glass, pottery, lamps, coloured woollen cloths and purple die found their way into the Fezzan in great quantities, and these expeditions may well have created opportunities for the peaceful penetration of the interior. As long as the system of frontier defences held good and the administration of the provinces remained efficient, equilibrium was maintained between the nomads outside the *limes* and the sedentary farmers within the provinces. From the middle of the fourth century A.D., however, when the Roman provinces were torn by religious schisms, persecutions and rebellions and ordered government became weaker, the raids of the desert nomads grew correspondingly more serious and frequent. The Mazices and the Austuriani, who were by now equipped with camels and therefore highly mobile, overran and plundered Tripolitania and the Cyrenaican Pentapolis. These attacks paved the way for the Vandal Conquest of the Roman provinces in A.D. 429, and continued during the Vandal period. They were succeeded during the next century by the even more fierce invasions of the Leuathae, who converged mainly on the western provinces. The Byzantine reconquest in the sixth century restored the balance temporarily and gave some respite to the battered provinces, but the impetus of Roman rule had spent itself, and the enfeebled country succumbed in the seventh century to the Arab invaders.

What survived from the Roman occupation? The answer to this question is difficult to find. The three centuries in which the Arabs consolidated their conquest of North Africa remain a period of great obscurity, but it would appear that there was no sudden break with the past. The Roman language continued to be spoken in scattered places and isolated Christian communities, still torn by their immemorial schisms, persisted as late as the twelfth century A.D. One of the most remarkable phenomena, however, throughout the whole of this long period we have looked at is the astonishing tenacity with which many of the indigenous inhabitants, the Berbers, retained their ethnic identity and freedom, especially those of them who lived in the remote mountain fastnesses and in the fringes of the desert, many of whom continued to live their traditional lives unaffected by the successive waves of invading immigrants. All over the North African littoral, the silent ruins remain as a reminder of the direct impact of the Greeks, Carthaginians and Romans. But among the indirect results of their presence, the Sahara trade routes worked by the desert nomads, continued to operate until the age of the steamship and the railway.

CHAPTER FOUR

The Kingdom of Axum

G. W. B. Huntingford

NEAR THE southern end of the Red Sea the land of Yemen in south-west Arabia faces the high plateau on the mainland of Africa which is now called Ethiopia. This plateau is separated from the Red Sea, however, by a strip of burning desert lowland, parts of which are below sea level. Moreover, in ancient times it had but one port of access, Adulis (Zula), a place near the modern Massawa, and on other sides could be reached only by very difficult land journeys. It was thus for practical purposes one of the most inaccessible countries of the ancient world, and has in fact remained inaccessible till modern times.

As far back as the seventh century B.C. waves of immigration from the already comparatively civilized Semitic people of the Yemen began to settle in the Ethiopian highlands, where perhaps two or three centuries B.C. they established a centre at a place called Axum. From this nucleus there eventually developed the kingdom of Ethiopia. The motive for this settlement was clearly trade, for the Greek document of the first century A.D. called the *Periplus of the Erythraean Sea*, or 'Directions for sailing round the Indian Ocean', tells us that the metropolis of the Axumites was the collecting centre for ivory brought from Inner Africa, since it was on a route leading from the coast at Adulis to the interior. These Semites from the Yemen when they arrived found the land occupied by people of Hamitic stock, the hot lowlands by nomadic pastoralists, the cooler highlands by peoples who practised agriculture. In this land the newcomers, who called them-

22

selves Habashat (from which comes ultimately the name Abyssinia) developed théir own language, Ethiopic, or Ge'ez as it is properly called. Though it is no longer spoken today, this is the language of the Church and of literature, as Latin was in Europe.

During the early part of the Axumite kingdom, and from at least the first half of the third century B.C., there was considerable activity on the part of the Ptolemies of Egypt along the African coast of the Red Sea, where they hunted and collected elephants for use in war. Much of this business was in the hands of Greeks, some of whose names are recorded in Greek inscriptions; and though these trading activities of the Ptolemies seem to have had little influence on the development or on the internal affairs of Axum, they did introduce Greek, as the language of trade and diplomacy. In fact, Greek was used (though perhaps sparingly) in official records up to at least the fourth century A.D.

Round Axum there grew up a number of small states, one of which soon became dominant and reduced the rulers of the others to the status ot tributary kings. These were left to their own devices so long as they paid tribute to the king of Axum. But if they failed to do so, or if they interfered with the king's trading caravans, they were punished. One of them seems to have been king of the coast-lands, and perhaps the Zoscales mentioned in the *Periplus of the Erythaean Sea* ruled here in the first century, a forerunner of the later official called *bahr nagash* or 'sea king', the governor of northern Ethiopia. By the fourth century these states were absorbed into the Axumite state, for they are not heard of again.

The kings of Ethiopia claimed descent from Solomon through Menelik his son by the Queen of Sheba, who brought the Ark of the Law from Jerusalem to Axum. There are detailed accounts of this in Ethiopic literature, but they are all pure fable and invention. Nevertheless, the kings did believe themselves to be the descendants of Solomon, and were even referred to sometimes as Israelites. But till the fourth century A.D., the Axumites were pagans, whose god was not the God

23

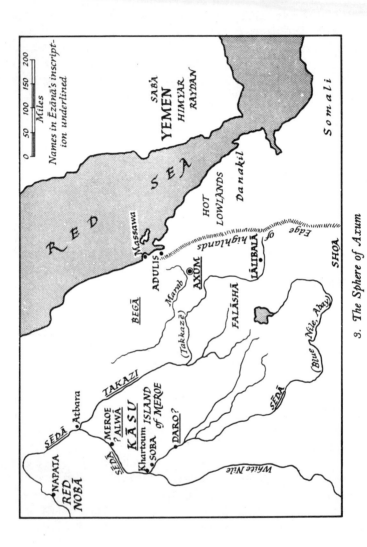

3. *The Sphere of Axum*

of Israel, but the gods of south Arabia. In A.D. 333 Christianity was introduced by a Syrian named Frumentius. According to both tradition and the Greek and Latin historians, Frumentius, after establishing the new religion, visited Saint Athanasius the famous Patriarch of Alexandria and was made by him head of the new Ethiopian Church. Hence, the rites and doctrines of the Alexandrian Church became those of Ethiopia and have remained so ever since. It is for this reason that the Ethiopian Church is often called Coptic. The king of Axum who was converted by Frumentius was called Ēzānā. After his conversion, Ēzānā made Christianity the official religion of the country, and it has continued to this day to be a force of immense power throughout Ethiopia, permeating all phases of Ethiopian life. The effect of the new religion is shown strikingly in the so-called Christian inscription of Ēzānā, who before his conversion began his official records (which were inscribed on stone) with the usual style 'King of Axum and of Himyar and of Kāsu and of Sab'a and of Raydān, king of kings, son of Maro the Unconquered'. But now there is an abrupt change, for we find instead the introductory phrase 'With the help of the Lord of Heaven and Earth, Ēzānā king of Axum, etc.', and there are further references to the 'Lord of Heaven' and the 'Lord of All'. This change of style is interesting in two respects. First, it shows clearly the abolition of a paganism dominated by the Arabian gods. Secondly, it is plain that we have here the retention of a string of titles which now had no political accuracy, but were retained from the previous century as traditional. For there is no evidence to show that any further attempts were made to reconquer the Yemen after the time of Aphilas till the sixth century, and the fairly numerous inscriptions of Ēzānā contain no reference at all to any activity there. The conclusion is that Axumite domination had ceased completely, and only the traditional titles remained to the Axumite kings as a reminder of their lost possessions.

On the other hand, all Ēzānā's inscriptions record wars in Africa. These records are written in Ethiopic, some with versions in Greek and south Arabian, and describe the suppression of revolts to the north and south of Axum. In addition, they mention Axum's western neighbour Meroe, which lay between the Atbara and the Blue Nile, and had grown from being a province of Egypt to an independent Africanized kingdom. In the Christian inscription there is a long and detailed account of a campaign in the Sudan. This inscription, omitting irrelevant detail (shown by dots, which do not mean gaps in the text) is as follows:

'With the help of the Lord of Heaven, who in heaven and earth conquers all, Ēzānā son of Ella Amidā, a member of (the group) Halēn, king of Axum and of Hemēr (Himyar) and of Raydān and of Sab'a and of Salhēn and of Tsyāmo and of Begā and of Kāsu, king of kings . . . never conquered by an enemy. . . . By the power of the Lord of All I made war on the Nobā. . . . I set out by the power of the Lord of the Earth[1] and fought at the Takazi, by the Ford of Kemalkē. . . . I burnt their towns, those with stone houses and those with straw huts; and (my troops) pillaged their corn and bronze and iron and copper; they destroyed the effigies in their houses (temples), and also their stores of corn and cotton, and threw them into the river Sēdā. . . . And I reached the Kāsu, whom I fought and made captive at the confluence of the rivers Sēdā and Takazi; and the next day I sent my troops . . . on a campaign up the Sēdā to the towns of stone and of straw; the names of the towns of stone are Alwā and Daro. . . . Then I sent troops . . . down the Sēdā to the four straw villages of the Nobā and the king. The stone towns of the Kāsu which the Nobā took (were) Tabito, Fertoti; and they (my troops) went as far as the Red Nobā. . . .'

From this it will be seen that Ēzānā went down the Takkazē, which eventually becomes known as Atbara and joins the Blue Nile, Ēzānā's *Sēdā* near Atbara; here, in the Island of Meroe, were the *Kāsu*, 'the people of Kush'. *Alwā*, up-river from Atbara, may have been Meroe itself (Shendi), though it has also been placed at Soba, twelve miles south of Khartoum. *Daro* seems to be the *Daron* of the geographer

[1]This expression, *egzi'a behēr*, became the normal Ethiopic word for 'God'.

Ptolemy, and perhaps Arbagi, eighty miles south-east of Khartoum. The *Red Nobā* are the Nubae of Strabo; they lived north of Meroe. *Tabito* and *Fertoti* are unidentifiable. This was in fact the campaign in which Ēzānā completed the destruction of Meroe, and was the culmination of a series of attacks by his predecessors. One of these, whose name is unfortunately missing from the record, left a Greek inscription in the city of Meroe itself recording his capture of the place.

It is somewhat remarkable that the kingdom of Axum, placed between the Ptolemaic sphere of influence in the east and Meroe in the west, acquired but little from these foreign cultures except the use of Greek for official records. The culture of Ethiopia was from the first of a south Arabian character which grew up with an atmosphere all its own. In its buildings, as may be seen at Axum and elsewhere, the architectural style is characterized by the use of stepped walls; giant obelisks cut into the shape of many-storeyed castles from single blocks of stone, including one 60 feet high; stone thrones; and embattled palaces. In the churches, too, the architecture is peculiar to Ethiopia.

In the sixth century the Yemenites began to oppress the Christians in the Yemen, and about 528 Kāleb king of Axum was fighting over there. The Ethiopians once more gained a temporary control exercised through deputies, but before long they were driven out, and this was their last Arabian adventure. During this period one of the local Ethiopian governors, named Abrehā, who had formerly been a slave, made an attack on Mecca. This was the War of the Elephant, so called through confusion with legends of an earlier king Aphilas who had invaded Arabia 150 years before, and whose name suggested to the Arabs their word *al-fil*, 'the elephant'. The result was to unite the Arabs and seal Arabia against Ethiopian influence for ever.

Then come the Dark Ages, of which we know very little but the names of kings. At last, however, there is a flash of light. Early in the tenth century a people called Falāshā,

Hamites who practised the Jewish religion, under the leadership of their queen, Esther, drove out the reigning dynasty
which claimed descent from Solomon, and after three years of
terrible misrule and destruction were succeeded by a new
dynasty, the Zāguē, who, as one chronicler says, were not
Israelites. The result of this was that the Solomonian dynasty
took refuge in Shoa, to the south, and Axum ceased to be the
political capital, though it remained (as it had been from the
beginning) the religious centre where the kings were
crowned; Ethiopia had in fact no permanent capital till
well into the seventeenth century. The dynasty which was
not Israelite held the throne of Ethiopia for 150 years, but
returned it to the Solomonian line in 1268. This, according to
the received story, was mainly through the intervention of
the great Ethiopian saint Takla Hāymānot, whose sanctity,
ability, and political astuteness achieved without the aid of
fighting a result almost without parallel elsewhere. Historically, however, the last Zāguē king was defeated in battle by
Yekuno Amlāk, the first king of the 'restored' line, who may
have been encouraged by another saint named Iyasus M'oa.
Though regarded as usurpers, some at least of the Zāguē
were Christians, and even holy men. One of these Zāguē
kings, named Lālibalā, was responsible for the making of a
number of rock-hewn churches at a place in central Ethiopia
which still bears his name. These churches are unique in their
design. They were made by isolating a block of rock within
a trench, which formed a courtyard; the rock was then cut
into the shape of a built-up church with all its architectural
details, the roof reaching to the original ground-level.

To sum up: the early history of Ethiopia, disentangled
from its mythical aspects, shows that a colonization of north-
east Africa stimulated in the first place by trade, was followed
by consolidation, with a series of attempts to regain control
of the Arabian homeland which finally ended in the sixth
century A.D. Mixture with the Hamitic population in due
course produced an Africanized Semitic type which, while
without any negro characteristics, differed greatly in most

respects from its Arabian ancestors, and showed itself willing to embrace Christianity at an early period, doing so with such thoroughness that the new religion finally permeated the whole social and political life of the Ethiopians. We have wandered a long way from Axum in time and space. The glory of Syon, as they called the city, has departed, leaving only the obelisks and the broken remains of palaces and churches. But during the first six centuries of our era were laid the foundations of an enduring Christian kingdom.

CHAPTER FIVE

The Invading Crescent

Bernard Lewis

THE ARABS conquered North Africa twice—the first time in the seventh century, the second time in the eleventh. The two conquests were very different from one another, both in the circumstances which brought them about, and in the long-term results which they produced. Between them they made Mediterranean Africa an Arabic-speaking, Muslim country, and prepared the way for the spread of Islam southwards to the Sahara and beyond it into tropical Africa—sometimes by trade, sometimes by war, sometimes by peaceful penetration.

In the early years of the seventh century a new religion arose in Arabia—Islam. Through the preaching and endeavours of the Prophet Muhammad, a Muslim community and a Muslim state were formed among the Arabs, and within a very short time after his death both were ready to expand into the world around them.

It was in the year 639 that the Muslim Arabs, who had already conquered Syria and Palestine, appeared on the eastern borders of Egypt. By 641 Egypt had been wrested from the Byzantines, and a treaty was signed whereby it was incorporated in the new Arab Empire. The great surge of conquest, which had already established the rule of the Muslim Arabs from Arabia over much of what is now called the Middle East, was still far from exhausted. From Iraq the Arab armies advanced eastwards across Persia to the borders of China and India. From Egypt they moved westwards, in a great sweep of conquest that was to bring them to the Atlantic coast of Morocco, and across the sea into Spain, Sicily, and even France.

The first Arab troops crossed the western desert from Egypt into North Africa in the year 647—six years after the conquest of Egypt. The first expeditions seem to have consisted of tribal levies, reinforced by military units from the Arab army in Egypt. As in other areas, these first expeditions seem to have been no more than forays for booty and captives. There was at first no plan of conquest or settlement. These came later and almost by accident, when the weakness of the resistance offered to the Arab raiders by the Byzantine defenders encouraged them to embark on larger and more ambitious projects.

The conquest is usually associated with the name of the famous general 'Uqba ibn Nāfi', who was appointed to the command of the Arab armies in North Africa in 663. By 670 he was able to found the city of Kayrawān, in Tunisia, the military and administrative capital of the Arabs in North Africa throughout the period of the conquests. From here they were able to pacify and occupy Tunisia, and extend their authority westwards into Algeria and Morocco. The conquest of North Africa, which the Arabs call al-Maghrib—the West —was long and difficult, for every step of their advance was bitterly contested. The hard core of resistance came not from the Byzantines, who were swept aside and expelled with comparative ease, but from the Berbers—the indigenous inhabitants of the country. In time, however, they were won over to the new religion brought by the Muslims, and in the early eighth century the Berbers joined with the Arabs in the conquest of Spain. They remained, however, a separate element in the population, with a different language, social organization, and way of life. Even after their conversion to Islam, they retained their separate identity, and not infrequently came into conflict with their Arab co-religionists.

The Arabs began to flow in from the East in great numbers, and every unsuccessful Berber rising brought a new wave of Arab reinforcements. The newcomers were in part

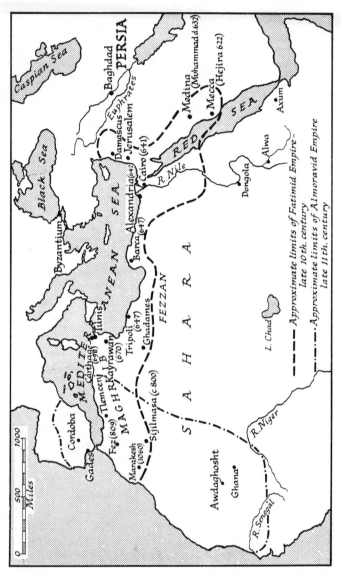

4. *Islam in North Africa*

tribesmen from Arabia, in part military units sent from the Arab armies and militia in Egypt, Syria, and the East. They settled in Kayrawān and other towns, which, as their population became predominantly Arab, served as centres for the Arabization and Islamization of the countryside.

The two processes were intimately associated. In the Arab Empire, the Arab town fulfilled several different but interrelated functions. Originally a military base and garrison centre, it came also to be an administrative and economic centre. Through the processes of government and the exchange of commodities, the Arabic language spread from the Arab masters to the large, non-Arabic population that thronged to the cities to serve their various needs, and then beyond them to the countryside.

Arabic was the language of both government and trade, with the usefulness and the prestige attached to them. But that was not all. It was also the language of religion—of the Kur'ān, the Holy Book of the Muslim faith brought to Africa by the conquerors. Contrary to popular belief, the Arabs did not impose their faith by force on the populations they conquered. The faith of the conquerors, however, spread rapidly, and with it the language of their scriptures and their religious learning. Not all the Arabs who came to North Africa were soldiers and administrators. Some were men of religion, who came to convert the Berbers to Islam, and to instruct them in the new faith. From the early eighth century onwards these became more numerous—and more successful.

There is one other element among the settlers from the East that should be mentioned—the merchants. In the early days of Islamic rule, North Africa was in effect a colonial dependency of the Arab Empire in the East, in which we can recognize the familiar pattern of soldiers, administrators, missionaries, and merchants. These last came chiefly from Syria and Iraq, sometimes from as far away as Persia and Central Asia. This trade was in various commodities. Some early Arab sources speak in wonderment of the vast forests of olive-trees which then existed in North Africa; others tell of the splendid horses and hardy camels of that country. The two most important exports to the East, however, were gold and slaves. When the Berbers became Muslims and could no longer lawfully be enslaved, other peoples, in the still unconquered lands to the south, were found to take their places. Gold came from West Africa, from the kingdom of Ghana, the capital of which then lay north of the Niger, and Muslim merchants from the Mediterranean coast-lands travelled for months to reach the great commercial centres of the south, where gold and slaves were to be bought. Some idea of the volume of the traffic may be gained from a remark of the Arab traveller Ibn Hawkal in the middle of the tenth century. He tells us that he saw a cheque for 42,000 dinars (gold pieces), acknowledging a debt of a trader resident at Awdaghost, in the southern fringes of the Sahara, to a merchant from Sijilmasa in Southern Morocco.

It was primarily for commercial reasons that the Muslims moved southwards into West Africa, and by the beginning of the eighth century they were probably already travelling and settling—as agents or buyers—in the market centres south of the Sahara. It was not until some time later that they began to seek religious converts, and then the missionaries were chiefly Berber.

For early medieval Islam, Africa was a colonial frontier, to which it looked rather as Europe looked to America from the sixteenth until the eighteenth or even the nineteenth century. At first it was the still unconquered West of Islam, offering the alternatives, equally seductive to different minds, of booty or martyrdom. Then, as the West was conquered and colonized, it became the land of hope and opportunity, where fortunes could be made, and where, in the freer spirit of the frontier, the persecuted and the unfortunate might hope to find a home and a refuge.

By the ninth century the Maghrib—the Islamic West—was rich enough and advanced enough to throw off the authority of the East and set up independent Muslim states. Arab and Berber dynasties arose in Morocco and Tunisia, which, while recognizing the nominal suzerainty of the Caliphs in the East, were in fact completely independent. At the beginning of the tenth century the Fātimids, though themselves of eastern origin, set up in Tunisia a real North African Empire, which for a while was able to unite North Africa and Sicily in a single state, and which by the middle of the century was able to sweep eastwards to the conquest of Egypt, Syria, and part of Arabia. By this time North Africa had become rich and powerful, and was expanding, militarily and commercially, into both Europe and the Middle East. The Fātimid Caliphate, even after its transfer from Tunisia to Egypt, was still for a while a predominantly North African state, with Berber garrisons holding Cairo and Damascus; its eastern conquests gave the merchants of the Maghrib the opportunity to share extensively in the trade with southern and eastern Asia.

Towards the end of the tenth century Muslim North Africa had reached the peak of its prosperity and power. In the following century two great changes took place, one of which was to bring almost complete devastation

The crisis of the eleventh century was one which North Africa shared with the world of Islam as a whole. In the east, Turkish invaders from Central Asia conquered the heartlands of Islam, and founded a supremacy that was to last for over eight centuries. In Europe, Christian forces reconquered much of Spain and Sicily from Islam, and by the end of the century the Crusaders were able to establish themselves even in Syria and Palestine. In Africa two important changes took place. A new religious movement had sprung up among the Muslims in southern Morocco and the Senegal-Niger Basin. This movement won extensive support among both the Berber and Negro populations of the area. In 1054 Awdaghosht, then subject to Ghana, was attacked and captured by the sectaries. Twenty years later they were conquering Morocco and preparing the creation of a great Berber Empire in the far west, stretching from Spain to Senegal.

Quite different in character was the invasion of Tunisia and eastern Algeria by the Banu Hilāl and Banu Sulaym. These were two great bedouin tribes from Arabia, who had settled in Iraq and Syria, and, by their raiding and plundering, had caused much trouble to the rulers of those countries. In 978, after an unsuccessful revolt against the Fātimids, they were deported to Upper Egypt.

It was from there that, in the eleventh century, they began to move westward to the conquest of Tunisia. By 1056–7 they were able to devastate the old Arab capital of Kayrawān. The movement of the tribes, which continued into the twelfth and thirteenth centuries, brought havoc and ruin to North Africa. The fourteenth century historian Ibn Khaldun, perhaps the greatest of Arab historians and himself a Tunisian, describes it in these words:

'In Tunisia and the West, since the Hilal and Sulaym tribes passed that way at the beginning of the fifth century [that is, the middle of the eleventh century A.D.] and devastated these countries, for three hundred and fifty years all the plains were ruined; whereas formerly from the lands of the negroes to the shores of the Mediterranean all was cultivated, as is proved by the traces remaining there of monuments, buildings, farms, and villages.'

The Hilāli invasions left Libya, Tunisia, and eastern Algeria permanently impoverished and enfeebled. They did not, however, affect western Algeria and Morocco, which now became the main centre of western Islam. Under the Almoravids and their successors the Almohads, Moroccan Islam entered on a new phase of development and expansion, of the greatest importance in the history of all North-West Africa.

CHAPTER SIX

Kingdoms of the Western Sudan

Thomas Hodgkin

THE SUDAN, meaning 'the country of the Black People', is the name the Arabs gave to the great belt of savannah stretching across Africa from the Atlantic to the Red Sea. North of it lies the Sahara desert; south of it is tropical forest. In the west the river Niger flows through the Sudan for most of its course, providing a natural link for the peoples who live along it. It was in this region that large, well-organized, predominantly Negro states—which at the height of their power could reasonably be called empires—were established during the period known to Europeans as the Middle Ages. Three of these states stand out in history: Ghana, Mali, and Gao.

Why were these states important? Principally because they played the part of middlemen. They were middlemen in the commercial sense: their towns were the great markets —for gold and slaves from the forest countries to the south; for salt from the Sahara mines; for horses, cloth, swords, books, and haberdashery from North Africa and Europe. But they were also intermediaries as regards ideas: from the eleventh century onwards the towns of the western Sudan were the main centres from which the teachings of Islam, carried across the desert from North Africa, began to be spread among West Africans. The spread of Islam meant a great deal to West Africa. Among other things, it meant much closer contact across the Sahara between the Arab and Negro worlds, and the growth of Muslim learning and scientific interests. Indeed, what we know about these kingdoms comes mainly from the works of Arab geographers, who were interested in describing this frontier Muslim region, or of Negro scholars writing in Arabic.

One way of looking at these Sudanese kingdoms is to take certain familiar dates in English history, and ask: 'What was the state of affairs in the western Sudan at this particular point in time?' This may help us to fit the rise, development, and decline of Ghana, Mali, and Gao into some kind of historical framework.

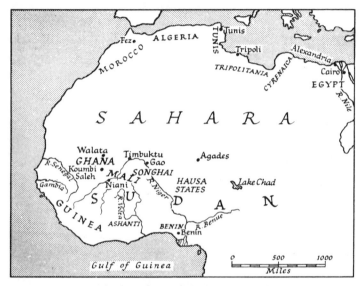

5. The Kingdoms of the Western Sudan

Let us begin with that well-known date, 1066. When William of Normandy invaded England, what was happening in West Africa? The most powerful state at this time was certainly Ghana, ruled over by a still surviving people called the Sarakole, which since the eighth century or earlier dominated the region north of the Senegal and Niger rivers. We need to remember, of course, that this ancient Ghana, on the edge of the Sahara, lay several hundred miles north of modern Ghana—the Gold Coast, as it used to be called. The main link between the two is that the people of modern Ghana, the first West African colony to become an independent state, look back to this ancient kingdom of Ghana as their cultural ancestor, rather in the way that modern Europeans look back to Greece and Rome. Much the best account of eleventh-century Ghana comes from the excellent Arab geographer al-Bakri, who completed his *Description of North Africa* in 1067. Though al-Bakri lived all his life at Cordova, in Spain, he must have collected information from merchants who knew Ghana at first-hand, as well as drawing on the Cordova archives. Here are a few sentences from his account:

'Ghana consists of two towns situated in a plain. The one inhabited by Muslims is very big and includes twelve mosques. . . . The town the king lives in is six miles away and is called *al-Ghaba*, which means "the forest". The territory between the two towns is covered with dwellings. The houses are built of stone and wood. . . . The king's interpreters, the controller of his treasury, and the majority of his viziers are chosen from among the Muslims. . . .

The religion of these Negroes is paganism and the worship of idols. . . . All the gold nuggets found in the mines belong to the king; but he leaves to his people the gold dust, with which everybody is familiar. . . The king of Ghana can raise 200,000 warriors, 40,000 of them being armed with bows and arrows. . . .'

Al-Bakri speaks here of the capital of Ghana as consisting of two towns—one Muslim, the other predominantly pagan. The site of the Muslim town is almost certainly the modern Koumbi Saleh, in the extreme south of what is now Mauretania, where recent excavations have revealed a number of well-built stone houses, with triangular niches in the walls and Koranic inscriptions on the plaster; a mosque; and several large tombs outside the city. Al-Bakri also makes clear that in his day the ruling dynasty was pagan. But ten years after our reference date, in 1076–7, the situation changed. The Berber Almoravids, puritan Muslim reformers from the western Sahara, who had already established their power in Morocco, attacked and captured Ghana, and converted the dynasty to Islam. This clearly was the time when Islam was beginning to spread throughout the western Sudan, as much as a result of the peaceful penetration of North African merchants and scholars as of the shock of the Almoravids' holy war.

Let us now jump nearly three centuries and consider the state of the western Sudan in 1346, the year of the battle of Crecy. How did things stand then? The Empire of Ghana had totally disappeared. Its power was finally broken by its southern neighbours, the Sosso, probably in the year 1203. Most of the Ghana merchants and scholars fled north to a new caravan city on the extreme edge of the Sahara, Walata—though there may have been some southward migration of the Ghana people too. By 1346 Walata, and Jenne on the upper Niger, were handling most of the trans-Saharan trade that had formerly flowed through Ghana. And Timbuktu, on the Niger bend to the east, was already at the beginning of its period of commercial greatness.

Politically the larger part of the western Sudan—from Senegal in the west to the Hausa states (in what is now Northern Nigeria) in the east—was included in, or dependent upon, the widespread Mali Empire. Mali, the kingdom of the Mandingo people, began to be a powerful force in the thirteenth century. But it was the great fourteenth-century emperor, Mansa Musa (*mansa* in Mande means simply 'emperor'), who succeeded in pushing forward the frontiers of the Mali Empire to their furthest extent; and who, by his magnificently equipped state pilgrimage to Mecca, by way of Cairo, literally put Mali on to the fourteenth-century European map. (A picture of *Rex Melli*, 'the king of the gold mines', first appeared on a Majorca map of 1339.) The lavish presents of gold which Mansa Musa distributed in Cairo, and their inflationary effect upon the currency, were remembered in Egypt long after the event.

The best first-hand account of the Empire of Mali in the mid-fourteenth century is by Ibn Battuta of Tangier, the most enterprising of the medieval Arab travellers, who had already visited India and China, Indonesia and Turkestan. Ibn Battuta arrived at Niani, the Mali capital, in June, 1353, and

stayed there eight months. His first impressions of the reigning Emperor, Mansa Sulayman, Mansa Musa's brother,
were not at all favourable. 'He is a miserly king,' wrote Ibn
Battuta; 'not a man from whom one might hope for a rich
present.' However, relations improved when Ibn Battuta
obtained free board and lodging during his longish stay; and
he gives a vivid description of the elaborate court ritual:

'The Sultan's usual dress is a velvety red tunic. . . . he is pre-
ceded by his musicians, who carry gold and silver guitars, and behind him come three hundred armed slaves. He walks in a leisurely
fashion, affecting a very slow movement, and even stops from time
to time. On reaching the dais he stops and looks round the assembly,
then ascends it in the sedate manner of a preacher ascending a
mosque-pulpit. As he takes his seat the drums, trumpets, and bugles
are sounded.'

Eventually Ibn Battuta came round to a very favourable view
of the Mali political system:

'The Negroes possess some admirable qualities. They are seldom
unjust, and have a greater abhorrence of injustice than any other
people. Their sultan shows no mercy to anyone who is guilty of the
least act of it. There is complete security in their country. Neither
traveller, nor inhabitant in it, has anything to fear from robbers or
men of violence. They do not confiscate the property of any white
man who dies in their country, even if it be uncounted wealth.'

Such a judgement could hardly have been passed on contemporary France or England.

Let us take as our last point of reference the year 1513—
the year of the Battle of Flodden, when Henry VIII was the
young king of England. What was the situation in the
western Sudan at this time?

The kingdom of the Songhai people, with its capital at Gao
on the middle Niger, which had been expanding during the
previous century, was now at the height of its power. Its ruler
was one of the ablest of the West African sovereigns,
Muhammad Askia, generally known as Askia the Great; a
former general in the Songhai army, who in 1493 had over-

thrown the last ineffective representative of the dynasty that had governed for eight centuries, and taken over power in Gao. Under the Askia dynasty, which ruled Gao through the sixteenth century—coinciding roughly with the period of Tudor power in England—the greater part of the western Sudan was again united under a single government. Indeed, the Empire of Gao at this time stretched a long way farther north into the Sahara, including the vitally important salt mines on the frontiers of modern Algeria, than ever Mali had done. In the east, Askia the Great occupied the powerful caravan city of Agades, which controlled the main trade routes to Tunis, Tripoli and Egypt; and in this actual year, 1513, he invaded the Hausa States—including Kano, today the commercial centre of northern Nigeria—bringing them, for a time, within the Gao Empire. But it was not so much in his military achievements that Askia's genius showed itself as in the efficient system of administration which he developed, with the support of the Muslim religious leaders and the merchants, as a means of unifying this extensive empire. A system of provincial governors was introduced, and a number of central ministries created—for finance, justice, home affairs, agriculture, and forests, as well as a distinct ministry for 'White People' (i.e., for the Moors and Tuareg, living on the Saharan frontiers of the empire).

It was a little after this date, 1513, that a young Arab—his full name was al-Hasan ibn Muhammad al-Wazzān al-Zayyāti—who had been brought up at Fez in Morocco, visited the western Sudan in the company of his uncle, on a diplomatic mission from the Sultan of Morocco to Askia the Great. Later, while still only in his early twenties, he was captured by Sicilian pirates and handed over to Pope Leo X, who encouraged him to write about Africa and baptized him, giving him his own Christian names—John Leo. Thus al-Hasan ibn Muhammad came to be known to the European world as Leo Africanus. One of the points about the Gao Empire at this time which particularly impressed Leo Africanus was the influence of its merchants and intellectuals:

'The inhabitants of Timbuktu are very rich, especially the foreigners who have settled in the country; so much so that the king
gave two of his daughters in marriage to two merchants who were
brothers, on account of their great wealth. . . .

There are numerous judges, doctors, and clerics in Timbuktu,
all receiving good salaries from the king. He pays great respect to
men of learning. There is a big demand for books in manuscript,
imported from Barbary. More profit is made from the book trade
than from any other line of business. . . .'

Timbuktu was the acknowledged intellectual centre of
Askia's empire. Its university provided courses in theology,
Muslim law, rhetoric, grammar, and literature, given by
visiting lecturers from Cairo and Fez as well as by local
scholars, and attended by students—'young men eager for
knowledge and virtue', as a writer of the day described them
—from the surrounding West African region.

Ghana, Mali, Gao: what—one inevitably asks—were the
causes of the break-up of these large, relatively centralized
Negro empires, and the flourishing civilizations associated
with them, after about the year 1600? Lack of natural frontiers—meaning exposure to attack from desert and forest?
Poor communications? Excessive dependence on the trade in
gold and slaves? The sharp contrast (which struck Leo
Africanus) between the splendour of the royal courts and the
poverty of the masses? To try to answer this question at all
adequately would take us too far. But in the case of Gao one
point is clear: the invasion of the empire in 1590 by Moroccan
forces, armed with harquebus and cannon, which had succeeded
in solving the problems of trans-Saharan transport, was the
beginning of a time of troubles. The old equilibrium—
between Negro and Arab, pagan and Muslim, settled and
nomad, city and countryside—was destroyed. As a seventeenth-century Timbuktu historian, who himself lived
through the troubles he described, expressed it:

'From that moment everything changed. Danger took the place of
security; poverty of wealth. Peace gave way to distress, disasters,
and violence. . . .'

Seventeenth century African writers, preoccupied with the political upheavals of their day, naturally looked back to the period of the Askias as a golden age. For the present generation of West Africans, involved in the building of new independent states, these Sudanese kingdoms of the past have acquired a new kind of importance, as a stimulus to future achievement.

CHAPTER SEVEN

The Land of Zanj

Gervase Mathew

THE DOCUMENTARY history of East Africa begins with a commercial hand-book of the early second century. It is written in Greek and called the *Circumnavigation of the Indian Ocean*. Now that I have travelled along nearly all the routes that it describes I have been convinced that it is the account of an eye witness. Sometime perhaps about the year A.D. 110 his ship, passing out of the Gulf of Aden, rounded the Cape of Spices that we now know as Cape Guardafui. He sailed southward along the shores of what are now Somalia, Kenya and Tanzania. He writes of the inhabitants of this area as savages but describes their markets as part of a close-knit network of Indian Ocean trade—ships sail there from Egypt in July, other ships come there direct from western India. There are Arabs who know the whole coast and speak the language. It is this coastal strip, stretching from southern Somalia to Tanzania, which came to be called Zingis or Zingion by Greek geographers and the Land of Zanj by the Arabs. Now the name only survives as Zanzibar.

All the East African coastline and its islands are littered with the fragments of ruined towns. It is only gradually becoming possible to disentangle the very different periods and cultures to which each belongs. Yet they have this in common. They all mark points of juncture where trade routes from inner Africa meet the Indian Ocean traffic that comes with the monsoons.

Such trade-routes were very different from those described by English explorers in the nineteenth century. In the late

6. *Medieval East Africa*

eighteenth and first half of the nineteenth century, Arab traders in search of ivory and slaves, penetrated far into the interior until at last they reached the great lakes. But there is no evidence that any Arab penetrated behind the coast south of Cape Guardafui until the second half of the eighteenth century. In the earlier period African traders came to the coast with slaves and ivory and they were stored at convenient centres by the mouth of a river or on some off-shore island, until they could be collected seasonally by the dhows that came south before the monsoon. This is, at least, the most probable hypothesis to suit such evidence as we possess. In one case, certainly, such traders must have come from a great distance. Gold and ivory were brought down from Rhodesia, and bartered at Sofala, a port in the Zambezi delta, in exchange for the Indian beads of which so many have been found among the Zimbabwe ruins. This trade-route down to Sofala and then by sea along the coast to Kilwa is of crucial significance for the economic development of East Africa. It is hard to tell when it began. There is some evidence from the *Chronicle of Kilwa* that the rulers of that small island-state gained a monopoly of the traffic in the late twelfth century. The gold trade seems to have reached its maximum extent during the fifteenth century, just before the coming of the Portuguese. No other trade route from the interior is of comparable importance. Dr Roger Summers has suggested that it is possible to trace a line of trade contacts from the Ziwa people in South Rhodesia, across the Zambezi by Tete, overland to Kilwa. Mrs Leakey has found cowrie shells from the Maldive Islands in an iron-age settlement near Nakuru in the Kenya Highlands, possibly these were the result of trade contacts with Malindi. Influences from as far north as Axum in Ethiopia may have reached south to Port Durnford (probably the Nikon of the *Periplus* and the Shungaya of African tradition) for I have noted a stela there which could be a link between the Axumite stelae and the later pillar tombs now so common along the coast. But when all this has been admitted there is still nothing to parallel the network of long trade routes of the early nineteenth century. Far to the north, beyond Cape Guardafui, the wealthy Muslim kingdom of Adal flourished in the fifteenth century, as the result of trade links that stretched westward to the Muslim kingdoms south of the

Sahara. Zeila was the outlet for Adal, and through it many slaves and some pilgrims reached Arabia. But with this exception there is no evidence for Islam in medieval East Africa except in the trading towns along the coast. Inevitably, the wealth and the importance of these trade centres waxed and waned according to the trade conditions in the Indian Ocean as a whole, for the Indian Ocean formed essentially one economic unit.

Right over on the opposite side of the Indian Ocean, I recently made an archaeological survey on the west coast of Malaya and I am now sure that there is the same rhythm in the history of Malaya and of the East African coast. In both cases documentary history begins with a list of small market towns known as far off as the Roman Empire but existing among a very primitive people only just emerging from the Stone Age. In both, the second period is obscure. It lasts from about the fifth till about the twelfth century. There is no evidence for any kind of contact with the Mediterranean world. Direct Indian influences were very powerful in Malaya, but possibly also in East Africa. Chinese trade goods and trade demands were beginning to affect the whole of the Indian Ocean. The third period lasts from the twelfth to the beginning of the sixteenth century. It is the age when the Muslims had control of the Indian Ocean trade. They came from Arabia and from the Persian Gulf and from Islamic India. Essentially they were trading as middle-men. In Europe there was an increasing demand for gold. King Henry III of England used African gold for coins struck at the London Mint, there was a steady demand for ivory, there was a rapidly growing market for every kind of spice. Muslim traders brought Rhodesian gold and Tanganyika ivory and Indonesian spices to Egyptian and Syrian harbours and so helped to found the wealth of medieval Venice and Genoa. Eastwards there was another traffic. African ivory was needed in China and much prized in India, while in Islamic India and in Mesopotamia there was an insatiable demand for slaves.

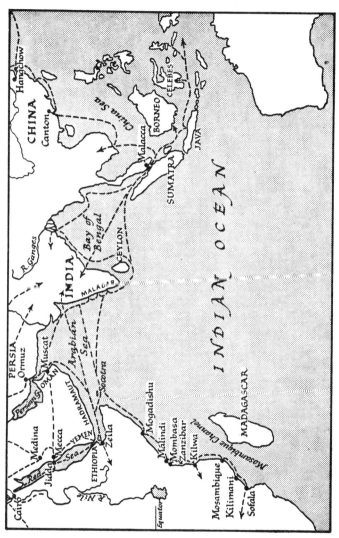

7. Trade Routes of the Indian Ocean in the Fifteenth Century

Our knowledge of this period in East Africa is increasing steadily through archaeology. Most of the medieval towns along the African coasts seem to have come into existence about the twelfth century and to have reached the climax of their prosperity about the year 1500.

Small trading towns, probably mainly built of wood, turned into great merchant cities, with their own characteristic architecture and with contacts throughout the Middle and Far East. In the ruined palace city of Songo Mnara on a coral island off Tanzania, each pointed arch with its thin stone edging is reset within a rectangle of cut stone, and fluted demi-domes rest on fluted pilasters. There is an intricate system of sanitation, with stone piping. Everywhere there is evident delight in geometrical precision. I found scattered among the ruins, broken glazed pottery from the Persian area, stone-ware from Burma and Siam, pieces of carnelian, and amber, crystal and topaz and a mass of Chinese porcelain from late Sung to early Ming.

There was a parallel development on the other side of the Indian Ocean. The fifteenth century cities of Kilwa in Tanganyika and Malacca in Malaya had similar functions as Muslim trading centres—it is significant that I have found not only the same types of porcelain at both, but in similar proportions. Even their organization was similar; much of the power lay with an hereditary 'Mayor of the Palace'; the Amir at Kilwa, the Bendahara at Malacca. The lost original of the *Kilwa Chronicle* seems to have resembled the early sixteenth-century *Chronicle of Malacca*.

Then suddenly the whole of that Indian Ocean world was transformed by the coming of the Portuguese. In November 1497 Vasco da Gama rounded the Cape of Good Hope and then sailed up the east coast on his way to India. Eight years later the Portuguese sacked Kilwa and Mombasa. For more than a hundred years they treated the Indian Ocean as if it were a Portuguese lake.

There are surprisingly few traces of this Portuguese period in East Africa north of Mozambique—a few fortifications in the coastal towns, some loan words in Swahili and perhaps an occasional custom like the bull-fights on Pemba Island, north of Zanzibar.

The Portuguese Empire could survive only as long as it held control of the sea routes. This was lost early in the seventeenth century.

The most flourishing of the Portuguese settlements in East Africa were destroyed in a revolt. Swahili states were able to come into being and to maintain a precarious independence.

This fifth period in the history of the East African coast lasted from about 1637 to about 1810. All down the shores of what had been the land of Zanj, there were small towns, oligarchic in social structure, trading in ivory and in slaves and using a currency of beads and rolls of cloth. All were consciously Muslim, all Swahili-speaking. The sites of this period are linked by the same type of house and mosque and fortification and pillar tomb and by the use of great quantities of Chinese blue and white porcelain. In the early nineteenth century their trade was sapped by the development of New Zanzibar under Arab rulers from the Persian Gulf. Now all are decayed and many of them deserted.

We can reconstruct much of the life in such towns from Swahili poems. It seems clear that though dependent for their wealth on Indian Ocean trade they still remained integrally African. Pate was perhaps the wealthiest among them—it became a proverb that the nobles there climbed by silver ladders into ivory beds, but we have a description of the rich men of Pate arching their long necks and swinging their many-jointed arms as the common people gazed at them, an African not an Arab ideal of deportment. There is much to remind us of West Africa. It seems clear that in each little state the Great Drum or the Ivory Horn were something more than ritual objects, in some fashion they enshrined not only the strength but the spirit of the people. Women were their guardians—they are perhaps the 'Queens' referred to in contemporary European accounts. Even the 'Decorated Ones', the courtesans, possessed a definite status. Witch doctors were potent and the religion of the coast though nominally Islamic was impregnated by the dread of spirits and of vampires.

If this was true of the seventeenth and eighteenth centuries it may well have been true in medieval East Africa. When the greatest of all travellers, Ibn Battuta, reached Tanganyika in the fourteenth century he describes Kilwa as a beautiful and well constructed city, but he also noted that its inhabitants were jet black and had incised their faces apparently for ornament. His detailed description of one of the Somali States suggests a Negro State like those that he had visited along the southern borders of the Sahara. No one can question the constant presence of Arab, Indian and Persian merchants in the medieval ports. We still possess the long genealogies by which the early sixteenth-century rulers of Kilwa claimed descent from Persian kings. But some at least of the cities discovered by the Portuguese may have been African kingships which had become Muslim and had slowly acquired the techniques and organizations of Islamic States.

Certainly to all medieval geographers the Land of Zanj is a land of Negroes. It is impossible to tell how long a form of Bantu had been the language of the coast but it underlies all variants of Swahili and back in the tenth century an Arab traveller had referred by a Bantu title to an emerald-crowned king of the Zanj.

But two things, at any rate, seem clear. The first is that the history of the East African coast only becomes intelligible when it is studied as a part of the history of the Indian Ocean. The influences that stimulated its cultures, like the wealth on which its towns were founded, came primarily from Eastern trade. But the second is, that it has always remained a part of Africa.

The Dawn came from the East, but it was an African Dawn.

CHAPTER EIGHT

The Riddle of Zimbabwe

Roland Oliver

AT ZIMBABWE, in the centre of Rhodesia, there are two
groups of stone ruins, which constitute perhaps the greatest
riddle in the whole of African history. One group crowns a
rocky out-crop, and might be a hill-fort. The other, in the
valley beneath, consists of a vast elliptical enclosure, mas-
sively walled in stone, with other stone walls inside, and in
particular a solid conical tower, which has no clear parallel
anywhere else in the world.

Who made these buildings, and when, and why?

The late nineteenth-century explorers who first reported
their existence to the outside world were convinced that such
things could never have been constructed by Africans. As
prospectors, themselves consciously engaged in the search for
King Solomon's mines, they attributed Zimbabwe to Phoenician gold-traders of the millennium before Christ. Scientific
archaeology has found just this grain of truth in their specu-
lations: that finds of Chinese porcelain, and glass beads,
apparently from India or Malaya, show clearly that the inhabitants of Zimbabwe, whoever they were, were certainly in
touch with the medieval trading system of the Indian Ocean.
There has been much rebuilding at both groups of ruins. The
earliest building took place on the hill-top around the eleventh
century. Parts of the valley ruins may be nearly as old.

Certainly, however, the builders were not the Phoenicians,
and even though they did trade with peoples outside Africa,
modern opinion is coming increasingly surely to the view that
the builders themselves were Africans. The Zimbabwe ruins

are impressive by any standards, but there is nothing tech-
nically very advanced about them. True, they are made of
stone. But this part of Rhodesia abounds in stone, and
stone-building of a kind is known to have been practised
there by Africans until about one hundred and fifty years ago.

8. *Medieval Rhodesia*

The stone used at Zimbabwe is neither exactly trimmed nor
bound with mortar. There is not the slightest sign that any
building there was ever roofed with anything more than
thatch or *daga*, a kind of rough cement made from pounded
ant-hills. There is no corbelling, no vault, no arch. There is
not a straight line anywhere. In fact, it looks as though the
general lay-out of at least the valley ruins is similar to the
grass and reed structures which formed the palaces, so-called,

of many an important chief or king in other parts of Africa. It seems, therefore, as though people accustomed to building in reeds and thatch, had simply translated their architectural notions, as far as possible, into stone—erecting stone walls instead of reed fences, and stone towers and platforms instead of artificial mounds of earth. The dwelling-houses, it seems, were made of mud or *daga*. That is not to say that the work was not carefully and resourcefully carried out—and on a scale that must have taxed the labour supplies of quite a large and well-organized state.

Of that state during the time of its greatness, when the original great Zimbabwe was still its capital, we know almost nothing. Only the evidence of the medieval Arabic writers and the physical remains of the Islamic merchant cities of the east coast, indicate something of the rich trade in gold and ivory that must have helped to swell its revenues. When the Portuguese reached the area in the sixteenth century, the kingdom was already in decline. The vassal states were falling away from their allegiance. The capital of the original builders had been moved away from Great Zimbabwe towards the north, out of the stone-building area; and it was constructed therefore only of wood and thatch. A new dynasty, called the Rozwi, had moved, or would shortly move, into the former centre of the old kingdom from the west, and it is to these people that we now know that we must attribute the later buildings at Great Zimbabwe, including the conical tower and the great girdle wall.

The new, northerly capital of the old kingdom was still, however, called Zimbabwe, and it was well known that former Zimbabwes had been built farther to the south, and of stone. The ruler himself was called the *Monomatapa* or, more familiarly, *Mambo*; and his people were known to the Portuguese as the *Makaranga*, a word which is still used to describe one group of the *Mashona* peoples of Southern Rhodesia. Even in the sixteenth century, the *Makaranga* were distinguished from the other peoples of the region by the fact that they were dressed in cloth, which was the principal commodity imported in exchange for the exports of ivory and gold. Altogether, there need be little hesitation in identifying the sixteenth century *Makaranga* as the descendants of the people who had built the original Great Zimbabwe anything from two to five hundred years before.

Who, then, were these *Makaranga*? To answer this question, we must look in more detail at what the sixteenth century Portuguese said about their customs and social organization. First of all, the *Monomatapa* was not what we understand by a monarch in the West, but rather a divine king or priest-king of a kind well known in certain other parts of Africa. His subjects approached him crawling on their stomachs, and I suppose that at formal audiences he sat concealed behind a curtain, for it is recorded that the common people, though they might hear his voice, could never see him. Among the courtiers, the king's slightest action was imitated by all. If he had a cough, they all coughed. If he sprained his ankle, they all limped. It was considered necessary for the well-being of the whole state that the king should be fit and without physical blemish. At the onset of old age, or if he developed any serious infirmity, he was supposed to take poison and make way for a successor. The religious observance of the *Monomatapas* was a kind of spiritualism, practised especially at the new moon, when the reigning monarch communed with his ancestors, who were supposed to take possession of the bodies of ecstatic mediums.

Along with the high-priestly notion of kingship went a well-defined and most elaborate arrangement of the court and the chiefly hierarchy. At the court itself the Portuguese observers listed a chancellor of the kingdom; a court chamberlain; a head drummer; a military commander; a keeper of the fetishes; a head doorkeeper; a chief cook; and so on. All these posts had special titles which passed from one holder of the office to the next. It was the same with the queen-mother and the nine principal wives of the king, each of whom had her own quarters and her own miniature court within the palace enclosure. Besides the official wives there were concubines and waiting-women to the number of about three thousand. And then, outside the court, there were the vassal kings, and the governors of provinces, and a large noble class, who were expected to send their children to be educated as pages and warriors at the *Monomatapa's* court. The key institution here was the royal fire, which burned so long as the king lived. All the great chiefs and other vassals had fires lit from the royal fire; and once a year, after the great new-moon ceremonies in May, these fires had to be rekindled from the central one. Messengers were sent all over the country with brands from the king's fire, and to accept the rekindling symbolized a renewal of allegiance to the king. When the king died, all the fires in the country were extinguished. On the death of a king, his spirit was supposed to take up residence in a lion, which for this reason was regarded as a sacred animal which might not be killed except at a hunt where the king was present. The king was indeed frequently referred to as The Lion.

Now all this is of the greatest interest, because it reinforces quite clearly the conclusions of the archaeological evidence, that the builders of Zimbabwe were Africans. There is no close parallel to the social structure described by the Portuguese writers, to be found anywhere outside Africa. But inside Africa there are several parallels which are so close that they cannot be co-incidental, which are indeed so close that there must be an historical explanation of them. The closest parallels of all are to be found in the kingdom of Ankole, in south-western Uganda, and in the former kingdom of Ruanda, now an independent republic. In both of these states every single important feature of the social structure of the *Monomatapa's* kingdom of the sixteenth century existed right up until the colonial period. In both these kingdoms you had the divine, high-priestly, self-sacrificing king; you had the cult of spirit possession; you had the transmigration of the king's soul into a lion; you had the royal fire and the new-moon ceremonies; you had the queen mother and the official queens with their courts; you had the office-bearers, the pages and the nobility of royal favourites. And all around, in southern Uganda, in north-west Tanzania, in Ruanda, in Burundi and in the eastern Congo, you had a whole collection of states which show in varying measure traces of the same influences.

What is especially interesting about Ankole and Ruanda, where the parallel is closest, is that you had there until quite recently visible, undeniable evidence of the presence of two communities, which had remained apart because their members formed two distinct social and economic classes in the state. There was an upper class of people leading the life of specialised pastoralists, herding cattle, living entirely on milk and meat, and disdaining all forms of cultivation. And there was a subordinate class of people who lived by agriculture. Though both communities now speak the same Bantu languages, the pastoralists have traditions of an original migraton into the area from the far north, whereas the cultivators have no recollection of having lived elsewhere. Physically, the pastoralists are markedly taller than the cultivators and most of them have sharp pointed features, more typical of the peoples of the Ethiopian region than of Bantu Africa. Zimbabwe, too, is set in typical ranching country, and a tenth-century Arab writer, in what seems to be a reference to this area, speaks of the great king of the Zanj as the possessor of vast herds of cattle, which were ridden by his soldiers in place of horses. Though we have no evidence as yet that the pastoral aristocracies of Ankole and Ruanda are as old as this, it is rather tempting to see this part of East Africa as a kind of half-way house for pastoral migrants moving down from Ethiopia into central Africa, and carrying with them a particular, rather characteristic version of African divine kingship, which blossomed in these widely separated regions.

About the motives of such far-flung migration we cannot yet be certain. Most likely, it is to be found in the natural increase of cattle, which have a habit of outgrowing the available pasturelands much faster than cultivating man outgrows the food-bearing potentials of the soil. More recent African history has been full of such pastoral migrations, and we know that the pastoral migrant, when he does move, will go fast and far before he finds the delectable lands where he will finally decide to settle. If he happens to come from a homeland where political institutions are well-developed, he will take them with him. But, no more than any other human institutions, will they last for ever. In Ankole and Ruanda, the peculiar culture of the pastoral immigrant happens to have survived until yesterday. In Mashonaland, it was already dying by the sixteenth century, and today nearly all trace of it has been lost in the culture of the agricultural majority into the midst of which it penetrated.

About the motives of such far-flung migration we cannot yet be certain. Most likely, it is to be found in the natural increase of cattle, which have a habit of outgrowing the available pasturelands much faster than cultivating man outgrows the food-bearing potentialities of the soil. More recent African history has been full of such pastoral migrations, and we know that the pastoral migrant, when he does move, will go fast and far before he finds the delectable lands where he will finally decide to settle. If he happens to come from a homeland where political institutions are well-developed, he will take them with him. But, no more than any other human institutions will they last for ever. In Ankole and Ruanda, the peculiar culture of the pastoral immigrant happens to have survived until today. In Mashonaland, it was already dying by the sixteenth century, and today nearly all trace of it has been lost in the culture of the Bantu majority into the midst of which it penetrated.

CHAPTER NINE

Peoples and Kingdoms of the Central Sudan

D. H. Jones

THE COUNTRY around Lake Chad has been called one of the great cross-roads of tropical Africa. It is an area where peoples of many different origins from north and east have been thrown together, and from which they have sometimes been dispersed again to the south-west and the south-east.

Eastwards and westwards, the open parklands, which are characteristic of so much of northern Nigeria, stretch almost unbroken from the banks of the upper Niger to the foothills of Darfur. There is an absence of natural barriers to human movement. Little groups of nomads, driving their herds of cattle and sheep with them, could drift, in a few seasons, half-way across Africa.

There are many features in the traditional religions and political systems of Nigeria which have struck some observers as evidence of the influence of the ancient Middle East, and it is true that almost all the historically important peoples of Nigeria possess more or less clear and precise traditions of having arrived in the land from that part of the world, from Canaan, from Yemen.

It would be a mistake, however, to understand these traditions as factual accounts of mass migration from the east in historical times. We should not picture whole nations on the move. Influences from the east have certainly been at work at various times in Nigerian history. The knowledge of iron-work, which was first developed in Africa in the neighbour-hood of Meroe, north of the modern Khartoum, probably entered from that direction. So did the traditional Nigerian method of casting bronze, the lost-wax process, which was originally invented in eastern Asia. The men who brought these crafts may well have brought new beliefs and institutions too, the early organization of Bornu and certain other Nigerian kingdoms was very similar to what we know of ancient Meroe. The fact remains, however, that in medieval and later times there was little direct contact between the Nigerian area and the Nile valley, while the recent discoveries of archaeologists have shown that central Nigeria was already inhabited, at least 2,000 years ago, by peoples of the West African Negro type who were, even then, not very different in their way of life from some of the simpler 'pagan' tribes of today.

The stimulus of new blood and new ideas came rather from the north by way of the caravan routes and oases of the Sahara.

Throughout history the parklands of the Sudan, their crops and herds and settled villages, have attracted the envy of the Berber and semi Arab tribes of the great desert. Time and again, small bands of nomads, better armed and disciplined than the Sudanese peasants, were able to set themselves up there as rulers of new states and to exact tribute from the settled populations round about them.

There were in particular two great political upheavals in medieval North Africa which started off powerful southerly movements among the Saharan tribes with consequences that can still be traced in Nigeria. One of the indirect results of the first Muslim conquest of North Africa in the seventh century was the foundation, about 800, of the kingdom of Kanem, to the east of Lake Chad, by a dynasty of White African origin. In the same sort of indirect way there may have been a connexion between the Bedouin invasions which disturbed the northern fringes of the desert in the eleventh century and the foundation of the oldest Hausa states. This second great period of unrest in the desert had certainly another and much more important outcome. It was at the

61

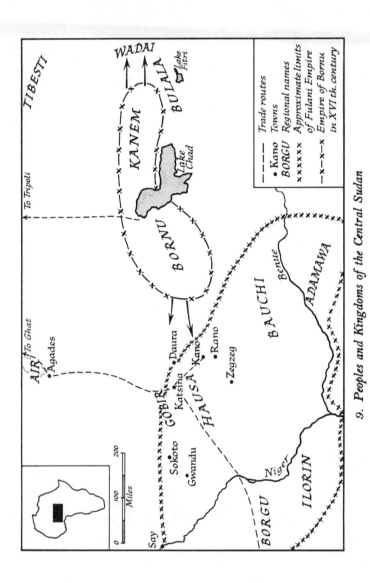

9. *Peoples and Kingdoms of the Central Sudan*

beginning of the twelfth century, with the conversion of the ruling dynasty of Kanem, that Islam first won a sure foothold in the central Sudan.

It would be almost impossible to over-emphasize the historical significance of the introduction of the religion of Muhammad. With the new faith came the knowledge of writing which made possible the growth of larger states and more efficient and systematic methods of government. It raised standards of morality and humanity and it established cultural ties between West Africa and the most highly developed of medieval civilizations.

The kingdom of Kanem, the first centre of this new civilizing force, reached the height of its fortunes under Dunama Dibbalemi (1210–24). Its power was greatly reduced in the course of the next hundred years by a series of disastrous feuds between members of the royal family until at the end of the fourteenth century Mai Omar found that he was unable to defend his frontiers against the rising power of the related Bulala people of Lake Fitri. He therefore transferred his capital to the rich pastoral country of Bornu, west of Lake Chad, and many of his still semi-nomadic people followed him. The sixteenth century was the great age of Bornu. Idris II (1507-29) reconquered Kanem, while Idris Alooma (1580–1617), the first ruler to import firearms (from Tripoli), completed the unification of the state, which for a short time extended so far eastward as to exercise some sort of dominion over Wadai.

Bornu was a conquest state, based upon the exploitation of a comparatively defenceless agricultural population by a small warrior class. It made very little difference to the age-old way of life of the village communities in which most of the people lived. For them the traditional headmen and elders remained in authority over everyday affairs. Great estates and provinces were parcelled out by the king for the reward of his principal ministers and war leaders, who regarded their lands simply as sources of tribute to be exacted by force or the threat of force. The king was accorded semi-divine honours. He lived amid great ceremony and in strict seclusion, making only rare and solemn appearances among his people. But he was no despot, since he was obliged to rule with the advice of the twelve principal officers of state and the effective core of the army, as in medieval Europe, was provided from the personal followers of the great lords. The basis of the economy was the slave raid. Every dry season the mail-clad horsemen of Bornu were dispatched upon slave-hunting campaigns among the less advanced populations to the south. Sometimes no doubt, the naked pagans, armed with poisoned arrows, were able to give a good account of themselves—the great Idris Alooma was killed by a hoe in one such skirmish— but commonly these 'wars' can have been little more than man-hunts. The victims made up the staple commodity of the trade with Tripoli and it was upon this link with the wider world that Bornu depended for the maintenance of its material strength and its Moslem civilization.

Between Bornu and Songhai on the upper Niger lay the fertile plains of Hausaland, dominated in turn by one or other of these empires but never falling completely within the political control of either. Here in the later Middle Ages there arose a whole series of small states, Daura (traditionally the oldest), Gobir, Kano, Rano, Katsina and Zegzeg (Zaria), which have been throughout their history more remarkable for the prosperity and industry of their walled cities than for success in war. They were probably offshoots of Kanem-Bornu and their political organization was of the same feudal type. The early rulers seem to have been of Berber origin. The Hausa language itself is classed by scholars as more closely related to Berber than to the other languages of West Africa.

The Hausa people are not a tribe. They have arisen out of the mingling, over the centuries, of many different tribal and racial groups which have been moulded into something very like a nation by their possession of a common language and their pride in a common culture. Yet they are not quite a nation. Their sense of unity was never strong enough to bring an end to the frequent petty wars between their little states and to unite them against their more powerful neighbours. The ordinary occupation of most Hausas is agriculture. at which they have attained a high level of skill but the towns were also busy centres of manufacture. There were easily worked deposits of iron in the neighbourhood of Rano and Kano and the founders of several Hausa towns are said to have been blacksmiths. Cotton was grown, and cloth-weaving and dyeing were important industries. Hausa leather-work became famous all over North-West Africa.

The Hausas are most adventurous travellers and merchants. Like Timbuktu, the Hausa cities were well-placed at the southern end of one of the great Saharan caravan routes, that which ran from Tunis through Ghat, Ghadames and the mountains of Air. When Songhai collapsed before the Moorish invasion at the end of the sixteenth century the main stream of trade with North Africa was diverted eastward to Hausaland. Katsina, in particular, rose to new prominence as a centre of trade and civilization. Hausa merchants came to control long distance trade all over the central Sudan. Hausa colonies grew up in all the important commercial centres and their language became the common speech of the market. Unhappily this intensification of economic activity brought with it an intensification of slave-trading and raiding in which the men of Zaria, the most southerly Hausa kingdom, were especially active.

Islam was first introduced into Kano by Wangara refugees from the west in the fourteenth century, but was slow to take root in Hausaland. Katsina was only converted in the course of the sixteenth century and many of the Hausa, even in the towns, seem to have remained virtually pagan for another 200 years.

The whole religious and political situation was completely changed by the Fulani *jihad* of 1804. The origins of the Fulani, a pastoral people who are certainly possessed of more non-Negro blood than most of the tribes among whom they have lived, remains pretty much of a mystery. In the first centuries of the Christian era they seem to have been living on the northern bank of the lower Senegal. Where they came from before that, and whether they were originally Jews, or Persians, or 'gipsies', are questions for romance rather than for plain history. At an early date they were beginning to move in considerable numbers into the lands of the Niger bend, and their peaceful wanderings with their herds had brought some of them through Hausaland as far eastward as Lake Chad and beyond as early at least as the thirteenth century. Many remained pagans and pastoralists, following the habit of life preserved to this day among the Bororoje. Others were already traders and town-dwellers and among these were Muslim scholars held in high esteem for their religious learning. They were an able, active people, unquestionably ambitious for political power, which their kinsmen in the west had achieved in Masina in the fifteenth century, in Futa Toro, on the Lower Senegal, in the sixteenth century, and in the highlands of Futa Jallon in the course of the eighteenth.

Towards the end of that century the Islamic world was deeply stirred by a widespread movement for religious revival. The rise of the puritanical Wahabi movement in Arabia itself was followed by a great expanion of religious orders like the Tijaniya and Qadriya in North Africa which could not fail to have a widespread influence in the Sudan.

In Hausaland the revivalist movement was centred upon the career as teacher and preacher of Usuman dan Fodio, a Fulani of Gobir. His growing prestige was regarded with suspicion by the traditional rulers of the Hausa States and the king of Gobir at last tried to put a forceful stop to Muslim missionary activity. Usuman's reply was to preach a *jihad*, a holy war for the expansion of Islam, which rapidly won the support of most of the Fulani communities in Northern Nigeria. This was not simply an intertribal war. In spite of the allegations of his enemies, it is certain that Usuman was sincere in professing purely religious aims and there were many Hausas among his supporters. It is equally clear, however, that the movement owed its success to the appeal which it made to the racial pride and tribal loyalty of the Fulani whom it raised, within twenty years, to the position of a ruling caste throughout almost the whole extent of what is now Northern Nigeria and the Northern Cameroons. Only Bornu itself under the fiery leadership of El Kanemi was able to withstand their assault.

The organization of the system of Fulani emirates under the suzerainty of the Emirs of Sokoto and Gwandu (between whom the Fulani dominions were partitioned in 1808) mark the first stage of the evolution of the Northern Nigeria which we know today, but they were never able to establish complete control over the vast area which they had brought under their influence. The pagan tribes of the broken hill country in Bauchi and Adamawa maintained their independence and frequently carried war up to walls of the Fulani towns. The representatives of the old dynasties which had been deposed did not everywhere give up the struggle, and the history of most of the emirates is one long record of revolts and campaigns. It would, however, be unjust and unscholarly to judge the administrative effectiveness or the cultural achievements of the Fulani order by the standards of the twentieth century. There is in fact little to support the view, widely held by the British at the time, that it was only their intervention, at the beginning of the present century, which saved the collapse of Fulani authority. On the other hand, it is certain that under their rule the life of Nigerian peoples was penetrated and shaped, as never before, by the faith, law and learning of Islam.

CHAPTER TEN

States of the Guinea Forest

J. D. Fage

IN ANY general view of the history of Guinea, the forested southern region of West Africa adjacent to the sea, from the sixteenth to the nineteenth centuries, two facts at once stand out. The first is that this was the period of the iniquitous Atlantic slave trade, and this the part of Africa from which came the majority of the Negroes taken by Europeans to slave on the plantations in America. All told, the Atlantic slave trade is believed to have transported to America something like fifteen to twenty million Africans, and of this number possibly ten million were drawn from the coasts of Guinea alone during the period of about two hundred years from about 1640 onwards when the trade was at its peak. We have no means of knowing what proportion a number like this might bear to the total population of Guinea at the time; but, bearing in mind that it was only young and healthy men and women who were valued as slaves, a continuing drain of manpower on this scale might be expected to have had most harmful effects, moral as well as material, on the life of West Africa. Yet, and this is the second outstanding fact, this was a time when there flourished in Guinea Negro kingdoms comparable with the earlier great empires of the western Sudan.

I wish to say something here about four of these states: the Oyo empire of the Yorubas, and the Benin kingdom of the Edo people, both in what is now Western Nigeria; Dahomey, which has lent its name to the modern French-speaking state which borders Nigeria on the west; and Ashanti, farther west still, in what is now Ghana. Other interesting

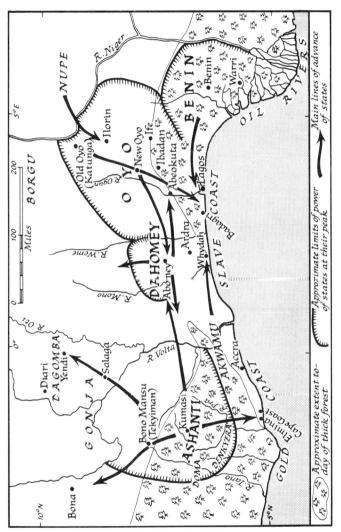

10. States of the Guinea Forest

states flourished in Guinea during the same period, for example, Akwamu, a predecessor from which Ashanti learnt much, but these four were undoubtedly the greatest. The slave trade definitely played a destructive part in their history, contributing to the decay of Benin, and, in the nineteenth century, together with the effects of the campaign against it, helping to disrupt the Oyo empire and to embroil Ashanti and Dahomey in fatal conflicts with European powers. Still it seems that in some way the slave trade must also have shared in creating political conditions encouraging to the development of states like these.

However, when, in the fifteenth century, European trade with the peoples of the Guinea coast began, Oyo and Benin, both offshoots of the famous culture of Ife, were already in existence. Oyo was one of a number of small Yoruba states, and one of the more remote from the sea, with its capital town close to the middle Niger, at the place now known as Katunga. We depend almost entirely on oral tradition for what little we know of its history at this time. Benin, on the other hand, lay close to the coast, between the Niger and modern Lagos, and in addition to its traditions we have, from the end of the fifteenth century onwards, valuable accounts of it from European sources. One of the earliest written descriptions, that of the Portuguese Pacheco Pereira, tells us of a walled city three miles long, the capital of a kingdom extending some two hundred and fifty miles from east to west. Pacheco says that this kingdom was usually at war with its neighbours, so that there were many captives for the Portuguese to buy. Clearly in fifteenth-century Benin a process of expansion by conquest was already under way. We cannot be sure what the causes of this were, but we can see that it had led to Benin City becoming the metropolis of a wide area. Thus it early attracted the Portuguese as a centre where their traders could expeditiously exchange their goods for the produce of the region, pepper and ivory and other commodities as well as slaves, and where their missionaries could with advantage preach the Christian word. European visitors continued to comment on the size of the city, its great streets and neat rows of houses, and on the enormous royal palace with its courtyards and galleries and its magnificent brass figures and plaques, until the middle of the seventeenth century, when a series of civil wars initiated a process of depopulation and decay.

The ostensible reason for this warfare and decline was a series of disputes about the succession to the throne. It is not unreasonable to suppose, however, that the underlying causes may be associated with the fact that it was just at this time that the European demand for African slaves entered upon its most intensive phase. It is known that the Benin kings had forbidden the export of male slaves (whom they doubtless required to maintain the strength of the kingdom). It is possible therefore that some of the principal men were now objecting to this policy. But there is evidence that many of Benin's earlier exports to Europeans had come from further afield, from Yorubaland. Here the state of Oyo was now expanding and, finding that it could not export slaves—now a principal export commodity—through Benin, began to send its trade to the coast further to the west. Thus the trouble in Benin may have been due to increasingly sharp competition for declining sources of wealth.

The little we know of Oyo before the seventeenth century suggests a state engaged in continual jostling with its northern neighbours, leading to wars in which cavalry were the outstanding arm; a state looking north, towards the Sudan, and not south, towards the sea, for what contact it had with the outside world. But in the time of King Obalokun, who must have reigned about 1600, tradition reports significant new developments: the introduction of proper salt to replace the inferior variety produced locally; contact with white peoples; and the beginning of conquests to the south. Now both salt and white faces could have come from the Muslim north, but the story that at the same time Oyo began to expand towards the south, into wooded country which presented its mounted soldiers with some difficulty, suggests that it was trade from the coast which had reached Oyo and had stimulated expansion in that direction. To the south-east, it soon became necessary to define a mutual boundary with Benin; to the south-west, by the end of the seventeenth century, the power of Oyo armies was being felt close to the sea in what was to become Dahomey. By the latter part of the eighteenth century, Oyo had acquired a large empire, and Lagos and Badagri were becoming two of the principal slaving ports of West Africa.

Immediately west of Yorubaland, Dahomey was originally the northernmost of a group of small states of the Aja peoples which were dominated by the kingdom of Ardra. In the seventeenth century, the increasing demand for slaves in the Americas led to a rapid development of European trade with Ardra and its coastal satellites, such as Whydah, which soon earned the sinister name of the Slave Coast. By the beginning of the eighteenth century, European influences were sapping the vitality and independence of the traditional modes of government among the southern Aja. This was not to the liking either of Dahomey or Oyo, both of which depended on the southern Aja for their links with the outside world. The kings of Dahomey had built up a much more effective and authoritarian form of government, and between 1724 and 1732, in a series of military campaigns, they intervened to impose this new order on the southern states, converting them into subject provinces. The evidence to suggest that they did this so that they themselves could the more effectively export slaves is at best inconclusive. Oyo, however, did want to export slaves, and objected to the whole Slave Coast coming under one potentially hostile military power. It therefore embarked on a series of invasions, which ended only when Dahomey agreed to recognize Oyo suzerainty. Ultimately, however, the Dahomey kings found that to export slaves was the best way to gain the guns and other European imports needed by their state, and, in the nineteenth century, with the collapse of Oyo power, they were raiding far into Yorubaland to obtain them on their own account.

Just as the power of Dahomey originated in reaction to Oyo aggression, so, farther west, in the forest behind the Gold Coast, the Ashanti Union was born at the end of the seventeenth century out of the coming together by a number of small states around Kumasi to resist the pressure of stronger neighbours, Doma and Denkyera. Ashanti tradition presents a picture in which astute statesmanship by Osei Tutu, king of Kumasi, and his chief priest, Okomfo Anokye, culminated in the recognition of the Golden Stool of Ashanti as the repository of a national spirit transcending all local ties. Through this and similar ideas, an *ad hoc* alliance of states became a single nation, a nation strong enough to absorb or to subjugate its neighbours, and then to advance to dominate the lands north of the forest. Whereas the expansion of Dahomey took place in the full light of history—it has been said that no West African road was more travelled by outsiders in the eighteenth century than that from Whydah to Abomey—the growing might of Ashanti was largely hidden from the white traders, marooned in their forts on the shores of the Gold Coast, until the middle of the eighteenth century, when Ashanti armies began a bid to control the coastal communities with whom the forts did their business. Nevertheless, bearing in mind the examples of Oyo and Dahomey (and of Akwamu too, for that matter), an economic motive for expansion is clearly suggested: Ashanti had won command of the trade of the hinterland, and then sought direct access to the coastal markets.

It would be foolish to suppose that the growth of these four great states was due solely to a desire to engross the trade in slaves. The origins of Ashanti and Dahomey both reveal the significance of local political factors, and we may suppose these also to have been significant at Oyo and Benin. Equally, these states must have possessed within themselves cultural and ideological seeds, such as the concept of divine monarchy that stemmed from Ife, or the idea behind the Golden Stool, vital enough to blossom out into complex and extensive systems of nation-wide organization and government. But it is

73

difficult to resist the inference that the operations of the Atlantic slave trade on the shores of Guinea had much to do with the timing and the shape of the rise of these states. Our modern concepts of humanity incline us, when we think of the slave trade today, to stress the word *slave* more than the word *trade*. But for all the great moral and material evil of the slave trade, we must not forget that the sale and export of slaves was only one half of the bargain. In return for the slaves they sold to the European traders, the Africans received not only firearms (and hence incidentally the means to build larger empires and to secure more slaves), but also many commodities which were socially more beneficial: cloth, tools, the raw materials for local smithies and workshops, and many other items of equipment needed by virile societies eager to increase their wealth and power under the stimulus of the contact with European culture and its ideas. It is true that West Africa paid for these things by exporting her people in a manner which we today can only regard as inhuman. But it may help to give a better perspective, if we remember that nineteenth-century Britain, while advancing to peaks of wealth and power unparalleled in her history, did so while no less than 19 million of her inhabitants were being forced, basically by economic pressures, to emigrate overseas, incidentally in conditions not so very much better than those in which the African slaves had been transported. It need not therefore cause surprise that the great increase of trade on the Guinea coast in the seventeenth and eighteenth centuries, even though it was occasioned primarily by the great demand for the export of labour to America, could have stimulated the growth of rich and prosperous new empire-states which, unlike their predecessors in the western Sudan, sought the commercial bases for their wealth and power by looking not north, towards the Sahara, but south, towards the Atlantic.

CHAPTER ELEVEN

The Old Kingdom of Congo

C. R. Boxer

THE OLD kingdom of Congo had originally extended along both banks of the River Zaire or Congo, as far as what is nowadays Stanley Pool; but when the Portuguese discovered this great river in 1482, the king of Congo no longer exercised any effective authority to the north of it. His capital was established at Mbanza Congo, some eighty miles south of the river and 150 miles by road from the sea. This place was approximately in the centre of the region which he still controlled, forming a rough square bounded by the sea and by the rivers, Zaire, Loje, and Kwango, respectively.

The monarchy was an elective one, but the absence of clear rules for succession to the throne led to the constant formation of opposing factions. Once established on the throne, the king theoretically enjoyed absolute power over the lives, lands, and property of his subjects; but in practice he had to pay a good deal of attention to the opinions of the leading nobles. The most important of these were the governors of the six provinces into which the kingdom was subdivided, and who were responsible for collecting and forwarding to the capital the regional tributes of raffia (palm-cloth), *nzimbu*, ivory, hides and slaves. *Nzimbu* were the principal form of currency, and the most valuable source of these sea-shells was the island of Luanda, which now forms part of the capital city of the Portuguese overseas province of Angola.

The Bantu tribes over whom the king of Congo ruled knew

75

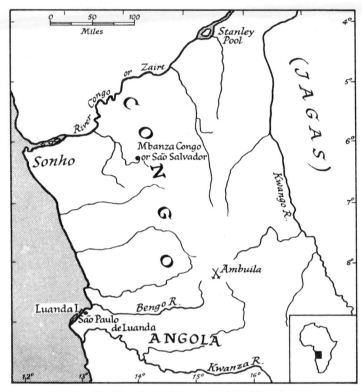

11. The Kingdom of Congo and its Neighbours

how to work metals, including iron and copper, and they were
fairly skilled potters. They wove mats and articles of clothing
from raffia tissues or palm-cloth, and their skill in this respect
excited the admiration of the Portuguese pioneers. They had
domesticated several animals—pigs, sheep, chickens, and in
some districts cattle, though they did not use milk, butter,
or cheese. They lived, for the most part, in huts or kraals constructed of flimsy materials and usually rectangular in shape.
Their agricultural implements were limited to the hoe and the
axe; but the millet and sorghum which they rather lacka-
daisically cultivated was supplemented by the fruits of the

76

forest and the products of the chase. Tribal law and custom regulated their daily lives, and the witch-doctors or medicine-men were held in great esteem. The Congolese did not know the art of writing, and seem to have had no contacts with the more advanced peoples on the upper reaches of the Niger, where there was a flourishing university at Timbuktu in the fifteenth century.

The Portuguese discoverers and pioneers in the Congo described the Bantu inhabitants of this kingdom as more receptive and intelligent than any Negro race they had yet met. Both traders and missionaries were warmly welcomed, and for a time at least the Congolese showed an enthusiastic willingness to adopt the ways of Western civilization which anticipated that of the Japanese 350 years later. This was particularly the case during the reign of Dom Affonso I from 1506 to 1543. As his name implies, this monarch was a genuine, fervent, and intelligent convert to Christianity, who did his utmost to implant the new religion in his kingdom both by precept and example. He wanted his people to adopt the European way of life as far as possible, and it seemed for a few years that they might do so.

The early Portuguese embassies and missions to the Congo included not only friars and priests, but skilled workers and artisans, such as blacksmiths, masons, bricklayers, and agricultural labourers. Even two German printers emigrated voluntarily to the Congo with their printing-press in 1492. History does not relate whether they printed anything in tropical Africa before they died, but a number of books, chiefly of a religious nature, were regularly exported to Mbanza Congo from Portugal. In the first flush of enthusiasm, several white women were sent out to teach the local ladies the arts of domestic economy as practised in Europe. A number of Congolese noble youths were sent to Lisbon for their education, where most of them studied at the College of Santo Eloi. In 1513, two scions of the Congolese royal house headed an embassy to the Pope, and one of them, baptized as Dom Henrique, was later consecrated Bishop of

Utica, at the insistence of King Manuel of Portugal. He returned to the Congo in 1521, with several other Negroes who had been ordained priests. He found that the work of propagating Christianity was being zealously forwarded not only by his royal father, but by an elderly aunt of 70, who was teaching girls in a special school.

Dom Affonso learnt to read and write Portuguese and he studied so hard that he sometimes fell asleep over his books from sheer exhaustion. He modelled his court on that of Lisbon and assumed regal styles and titles adapted from those used by the contemporary Portuguese kings. He established a Portuguese secretariat, and imitated Portuguese etiquette and dress as far as practicable. But his admiration and zeal for Western ways was not uncritical. He studied the Portuguese codified laws in the original bulky folios, and criticized the excessive penalties which were inflicted for even trivial offences. He jokingly asked the Portuguese envoy one day: 'Castro, what is the penalty in Portugal for anyone who puts his feet on the ground?' He supervised the building of a cathedral and other stone churches in his capital, and encouraged the erection of humbler wooden churches and schools throughout his kingdom. Mbanza Congo, now renamed São Salvador, was popularly termed in the vernacular *ekongo dia ngungo*, 'the town of the church bells'. Although much of his work died with him, his memory was kept green. A Roman Catholic missionary in the Congo wrote in 1889: 'A Negro of the Congo knows the names of only three kings—that of the reigning monarch, that of his predecessor, and that of Dom Affonso I.'

During this period, and indeed for long afterwards, the Portuguese did not attempt to secure political control of the kingdom, or to assert their influence by force of arms. The policy of their kings can justly be described as an enlightened one in this respect. They were, of course, anxious to christianize and civilize the Congolese according to Western ideas. But they strove to do this through missionaries, diplomatic envoys, and visiting technicians, and they treated the king of Congo as an ally and not as a vassal. What, then, prevented this Bantu kingdom from becoming westernized four and a half centuries ago, when the reigning European and African monarchs both regarded this as a consummation devoutly to be wished?

The reasons were many and various, and can only be summarized very briefly here, since this essay is not so much concerned with what the Portuguese did in the old kingdom of Congo but with what they found there, and what they thought of it. In the first place, there were never enough missionaries and technicians to teach the Congolese effectively. Dom Affonso repeatedly pleaded for many more to be sent him, but nothing like a sufficient number ever came. Most of those who did come soon died, like the German printers, in the tropical climate; as nothing was then known of the origin and cure of malarial fever and other tropical diseases. Secondly, many of those who came were unsuitable types with no true sense of vocation, for clerical morality in Portugal, as elsewhere in early sixteenth-century Europe, was at a deplorably low ebb. Thirdly, Portugal's vast and ever-increasing overseas commitments after the discovery of the sea-route to India and the Spice Islands, the fighting in Morocco, and in due course the effort to colonize Brazil, inevitably distracted attention and effort from the Congo. King John III of Portugal, who ruled from 1521 to 1557, unlike his two predecessors, showed very little interest in the promising Congo mission-field. He often left unanswered for years on end the repeated letters, pleas, and requests from the king of Congo and when he did send help or a reply of any kind, it was usually too little and too late. But the chief reason for the ultimate failure of the promising start made by Western civilization in the Congo was undoubtedly the close connexion which speedily grew up between the missionary and the slave-trader. That is another story, which I cannot develop here, nor can I do more than mention other contributory causes, such as the deep-rooted practices of polygamy and fetishism, and the devastation wrought by the

79

periodic invasions of the Jagas—wandering cannibal hordes of uncertain origin, who destroyed São Salvador in 1568.

Despite these drawbacks, and other handicaps which could be mentioned, the work of Dom Affonso and the Portuguese pioneers was not destroyed in a day, or even in a generation. From the accounts of the old kingdom of Congo given by later European residents and visitors, such as the Portuguese merchant Duarte Lopes, in 1588, and some Italian Capuchin friars in 1649, we can see that the 'town of the church bells' long continued to deserve this name. Lopes estimated the population of the capital at 100,000 souls, though the royal palace and the cathedral were the only substantial buildings, and the houses were mud huts thatched with reeds. These later observers, like the fifteenth-century pioneers, considered the Muxi-Congo, as they called them, to be physically and intellectually superior to all other Negroes. The Italian Capuchins were particularly impressed by the philosophical cheerfulness of the people in their daily life, and by their genuine unconcern for the acquisition of wealth and worldly goods. They still had only their rather primitive agricultural methods, but they now cultivated maize, manioc, citrus fruits, potatoes, and other plants introduced by the Portuguese. Some of their warriors had learnt how to use muskets, but the king would only allow these weapons to be employed by his bodyguard and by the defenders of the eastern marches against the incursions of the Jagas. The king and his court continued to dress largely in the Portuguese fashion, and corresponded intermittently with the monarchs of the Iberian Peninsula and with the Pope. Justice was dispensed orally in accordance with tribal law and custom, so far as the natives were concerned. Litigation between a Portuguese and a Congolese was decided by a resident Portuguese magistrate if the plaintiff was an African, and by a Negro judge if the plaintiff was a European.

The kings of Congo were mostly devout, if not strictly orthodox, Roman Catholics, but their relations with the Portuguese of Angola steadily worsened throughout the seventeenth century and eventually culminated in open warfare. Even so, though they allied themselves with the Dutch who occupied Luanda from 1641 to 1648, they resolutely rejected the Calvinist propaganda of their Protestant allies. The Dutch, incidentally, also bore testimony to the exceptional intelligence of the Congolese, and to the fact that many of them spoke, read, and wrote Portuguese fluently. The real decline of the Congo kingdom dates from the Battle of Ambuila in 1665, when the king was killed in a conflict with the Portuguese, in which both sides fought under the banner of the Cross. This ushered in a long period of anarchy, and by the end of the eighteenth century few traces remained of Congo's former Christianity, and the kingdom had shrunk to a small region around the ruined town of São Salvador. Even today this place is little more than a sleepy village, and the visitor finds it difficult to visualize the remarkable experiment of transplanting a European culture to tropical Africa which started there 450 years ago.

CHAPTER TWELVE

South of the Congo

J. Vansina

THE HEART of Central Africa is covered with huge forests threaded only by winding rivers which flow lazily towards the stream of streams, the River Congo. This area is inhabited by small tribes who have never been able to unite themselves in states and seem to have lived for many a century in the way they still do. Their only history is one of migrations of small parties groping their way through the forest. But this is only one face of Central Africa. South of the forest a large belt of savanna stretches itself from the west coast to the lake region. The rolling plains are covered with tall grasses and in the valleys the rivers are fringed with woods. Here man can move easily and here chieftaincies and kingdoms have flourished for some centuries. The kingdom of Congo, or Kongo, is one of these. It had however a particular destiny because of its contact with the Portuguese in and after the fifteenth century, whilst the states east of the River Kwango were not under direct European influence before Stanley's time.

During the Middle Ages or maybe earlier, a state existed near Lake Kisale, at the headwaters of the River Congo. Archaeologists have discovered there a cemetery which stretches for miles along the bank of the river. The dead were buried with their vessels and their ornaments. These include copper and iron objects such as belts, pins, and already the so-called Katanga cross. This is a copper cross which has long been in use as a currency. The finds show that even at that time the deposits of the Copper Belt were already worked by man and that some trade existed in the area. Moreover the size of the cemetery witnesses to the fact that this must have been the heart of a kingdom as the oral tradition of the Luba tribes, who inhabit the area has always claimed.

The traditions assert that the first kingdom originated in the Kisale area. Its inhabitants were Luba, but the rulers were Songye, a tribe now living in the east of the Kasai province. After some time the Luba freed themselves from the Songye yoke and started the so-called second Luba empire. Gradually

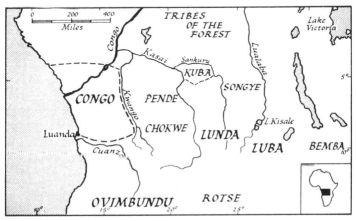

12. *Peoples of West Central Africa*

this state extended over most of Katanga. At the same time the Luba brought the idea of kingship and the techniques for organizing a state to their neighbours, the Lunda. All this happened at some time before the seventeenth century. During the seventeenth century the Lunda founded a vast empire. It stretched from the Kwango River in the west to Lake Moero in the east and it covered vast tracts of territory in Angola, Zambia, Katanga and Kwango. Moreover Lunda people sired the Rotse kingdom in Zambia, the chiefdoms of the Ovimbundu in Angola and many smaller states in the Kwango area of the Congo. By the end of this period the whole savanna was permeated with Luba-Lunda states.

This political evolution favoured the birth of long-range

trading routes from Loanda on the west coast to the heart of the Lunda empire in Katanga and from there to Lake Moero and the east coast in the region of Mozambique. Other roads linked the Copper Belt and the salt-deposits of Katanga not only with the centres of the Luba and Lunda empires but also with the smaller chiefdoms of Kasai. The traders carried with them most of the American crops the Portuguese had introduced into Africa and thus maize, groundnuts, tomatoes, tobacco and so on, found their way into the whole interior of Africa, and manioc became the staple food of most of these peoples. But not only did European culture traits travel along these routes. Elements of the different local cultures were also diffused and became accepted in other areas.

In the following centuries the role of these trade routes became even more important. Half-caste traders, called Pombeiros by the Portuguese, introduced more and more European commodities and the tribes which were living on the fringes of the Portuguese settlements in Angola became more and more acculturated. The Ovimbundu eventually secured a monopoly for the trade in the interior and a new nation called the Chokwe eventually succeeded with the aid of guns in overturning the Lunda empire in the late nineteenth century. But the Lunda recovered and were able to free their homeland. The Luba empire was overthrown at about the same time by a body of gun-equipped warriors who had come from the shores of the Lake Victoria Nyanza in Tanzania. They had followed a trade route and their superior weapons enabled them to achieve this feat. Soon after these happenings, however, the Europeans themselves appeared in these countries and divided them amongst themselves.

Luba–Lunda culture had thus spread over a very large area. But on the borders between the forest and the savanna their cultural influence remained small. Here on the rivers Kasai and Sankuru, on the fringes of the forests, lived a series of small peoples organized in petty chiefdoms. One of these succeeded in growing into a kingdom with a culture of its own, a culture which was in many ways more refined and fascinating than that of the Luba–Lunda. It is the kingdom of the Kuba and its history is fairly well known. We outline it here to show how an African culture develops itself both through acceptance of foreign culture traits and through internal evolution.

Most of the Kuba came originally from the central part of the west coast, from the region now called Gabon. When the Portuguese landed in the Lower Congo they fled to the region east of Stanley Pool, where they settled down in small fishing camps and hunting villages until the middle of the seventeenth century. Then they had to flee from the warlike bands of the Jagas who afterwards invaded the kingdom of Kongo. The fishers fled upstream and halted in the country between the rivers Kasai and Sankuru. The hunters came overland and reached the same area. And from the seventeenth century onwards it is here that a new state arises.

At their arrival the people lived mainly from hunting, gathering and fishing, although they grew some bananas. They learned to cultivate millet from the aboriginal population which they found there, but they did not take wholeheartedly to the cultivation of this crop. They knew iron and even copper, which they probably got already at that time from the ores of the Lower Congo. It is possible that they knew also how to weave raffia but this is doubtful as tradition has it that they wore bark-cloth garments. They were organized in small groups. One of these, the Bushong, had elected during their migration a 'captain of canoes'. Once settled down, his descendants became kings. At first the king was elected by the heads of the clans who had been his companions on the journey and they had power to depose him when they wanted. He was only a *primus inter pares*. But soon an internal development led to the emergence of a true kingship. The office became hereditary in one branch of a family, rules of succession were evolved, the deposition of rulers became impossible, a state-ceremonial developed, the clan elders had to swear an oath of allegiance to the king at investiture and to give him a wife as a token of this. Next, a system of tribute was developed, the collegiate group of elders evolved into a series of councils, formal offices were created and the title-holders nominated by the king and so on. At the same time a small territorial expansion brought the central region of the present Kuba area under control of the new state.

A second phase in Kuba history opens with the successful invasion of another Kuba tribe who destroyed the Bushong capital and killed the king. During the confusion which followed an adventurer, Shyaam a Mbul a Ngoong, usurped the kingship and reorganized the state. Shyaam had lived some time in the Kwango and brought with him a series of culture elements from that region. He introduced the American crops, especially maize, which became the staple food, with the result that the population showed a marked increase during the following decades. Further he spread the knowledge of different techniques in such industries as weaving and wood-carving. He sponsored over-production, markets and trade, even over long distances. The upshot of this action was a complete renewal of the culture. It was at this time that the Kuba developed their peculiar and artistically-minded civilization.

Shyaam's action in the political sphere was based mainly on the introduction of initiation-rites for boys, which were taken from the Lunda area. His own innovation was to concentrate the initiations at the capital and to keep the boys there for a year on military duty. He also invented a system of concentrating a large population in the capital so that the able-bodied men there formed an army much stronger than any which the petty chiefdoms surrounding the Bushong could oppose to him. No wonder then that he and his successors incorporated all the surrounding tribes in the kingdom. The Bushong invented then a method of indirect rule and created a state governed by a king, but with all the characteristics of a federation of chiefdoms. A last major change during this period was the transformation of the Bushong king into a divine king, a 'God on earth'. Appropriate ritual developed along with the change in the ideas about kingship. The whole system therefore seems to be of Lunda or Kongo origin, but with a considerable measure of local evolution.

On the close of the seventeenth century this renovation of the culture came to an end and a stabilization set in. The main reasons for this would seem to be, first, the fact that expansion had ceased because of the desire of the people to have the peace they needed for a flourishing trade, next the internal dissensions within the royal family, and finally the invasion of the Kasai by Luba groups who had been driven out of Katanga by the Luba emperors. During this period trade went on as before and the Bushong traded farther and farther afield, by land and by water. They reached the Lunda, Chokwe, Ovimbundu, Luba of Katanga, Songye and the peoples of the forest. They were also in contact with the Kongo of Stanley Pool and by 1850 they were known in Loanda.

The general political structure of the state and the legal system were completed and consolidated. The kingdom was on the whole peaceful, and this induced many foreigners of different origins to settle in the country, bringing with them all kinds of new culture-elements of lesser importance which became slowly woven into the fabric of the civilization.

This went on until the advent of the Europeans in 1880 and the following years. Then came the downfall. In 1904 the Bushong waged a war against the Independent Congo State and lost it. The country was brought under regular control about 1910.

We are well-informed on the Kuba of this period through the writings of Torday, an anthropologist who visited them in 1907. He hailed their culture as a superior civilization. And indeed there is some truth in it. The Kuba had one of the outstanding political structures of the continent, their arts rank very high and some of their carvings can be compared with Benin sculptures. Their economic development was remarkable and their religion highly sophisticated. This cultural superiority explains a last historical fact: their stubborn keeping to their own values and ways of life in a twentieth century of which they have only accepted the technical and economic aspects.

87

CHAPTER THIRTEEN

South of the Limpopo

W. M. Macmillan

SOUTH of the Limpopo means also south of the tropics, or, near enough, what is now the Republic of South Africa. The Limpopo shows on the map as a pronounced loop running, from nearly half-way across the continent, first north by east, then east by south, to its outlet in the Indian Ocean near Delagoa Bay. It is the boundary separating the Republic from Rhodesia in the far north, and from Botswana, the former Bechuanaland Protectorate, to the west. All the country in the same latitude west of the Limpopo (the Kalahari, that is to say, and South-West Africa) is arid and very sparsely populated, whereas the area embraced by the Limpopo includes certainly the richest and also many of the most highly developed parts of the present-day Republic of South Africa.

This southern region has no recorded history whatever before its discovery by Portuguese sailors in the late fifteenth century and very little, even then, till after the mid seventeenth century when the first handful of Europeans settled in its extreme south-western corner. At that time nothing was known of the Negroid peoples we know as the essential Africans, certainly not about their numbers, hardly even their whereabouts. The scouts of the European newcomers and those of these Bantu-speaking tribesmen first encountered each other only about 1702 a little to the west of Algoa Bay (Port Elizabeth); the 'Kaffirs' (as they were long called) were probably not in full occupation so far south as this point and certainly never beyond it to the south or west. There is no

doubt, however, that to the north and east they and their kin
were either in unchallenged occupation or free to roam at will
as they did over the so-called 'High Veld' plateau, the region
of the later Boer Republics, the Orange Free State and the
Transvaal. Any land remaining to the Bantu in geographically favoured parts like the Transkei and Natal is, much of it,

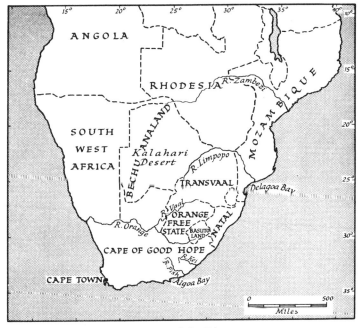

13. South of the Limpopo

acutely over-crowded. The High Veld, having a dry and even
very cold winter, was always less attractive to them and
except on its low-lying fringes, little has remained to them
except the also over-crowded mountainous knot now known as
Lesotho. Many South African historians and theorists have
made much of a claim that little of the area of the Republic
has ever been African territory and that what the tribes still
hold has more favourable natural conditions than anything

except the site of the original European settlement, the small south-western corner near Cape Town.

The distribution of whatever people there were, their way of life, and all the subsequent development of the South African story, demand a constant awareness of geographical influences. The rainfall, and especially its unreliability, was always a decisive factor, determined by the prevailing winds, the 'south-east trade', and the 'return-trade' or 'nor-wester'. Along the East African coast, south of the Equator, the 'south-easter' blows straight on shore and the mountain escarpment precipitates moisture from the warm sea air striking against it. This region is thus relatively humid and productive, and probably it has long been the main centre of the Bantu population. Late in the day, in the 1820s, a considerable upheaval in the Zulu country of Natal had repercussions far beyond its point of origin, and for the first time wars, associated with the name of the formidable Zulu, Shaka, came near to going on record; reliable witnesses saw and wrote some account of the dispersal of tribes which undoubtedly resulted. Only then we begin to hear a little not only about 'Kaffirs' and Zulus, but also, and virtually for the first time, of important tribal groups in the central or Limpopo area—the Basuto, for example, and their near relations, the Tswana; others like the Bavenda and the Herero become known to history only still later. Of all these groups, the Tswana in particular are assumed to have been 'driven' to the highly arid country which is now theirs; knowing this country fairly well, I have always felt that their skill, if only in hut-building, points to their having once lived in easier surroundings. Here again the common view of South African theorists fails to meet the facts. Building on their own theory that the ferocious upheaval due to Shaka was wholly typical, and at the same time completely ignoring the effects of the steady pressure on the tribes from advancing colonists, their bald assertion is that the southern tribes were themselves the advance guard of a mass migration from the north, their whole history in fact a long series of upheavals. Whatever else they were, these tribes were tough, as primitive peoples go: they had domesticated animals and grew food like millet for themselves. They are still notably cheerful and humorous and have successfully survived the many shocks and stresses they were to meet in the 'colonial' nineteenth century.

It was, however, from the south-west of the sub-continent that this phase of history took its shape. There totally different conditions produced very different people and made against any free coming and going. From about Mossamedes in Angola to very near Cape Town both 'south-easter' and 'nor-wester' are *land* winds all the way—and a cold Antarctic sea-current further reduces the humidity, often to zero point. Even people who know all about the Sahara in the north tend to forget the narrower but even longer stretch of unrelieved desert which bars any approach to the interior from the south-west. The country thus situated, being arid throughout, could support only a scanty population. Till Europeans arrived by sea, any people that were there could have no visitors, none therefore with wider experience to help them in their struggle for existence. The aborigines, accordingly, were primitive—even highly so. First, there were the little Bushmen—they lived chiefly by hunting. It is true they were naturalists: deadly poisons got from plants or insects made their arrows fatal to game. They also had skill in drawing and painting: their rock paintings are still to be seen in places whence Bushmen have long since vanished. But having no power of adapting themselves they have all but died out, except (in dozens) in the remotest Kalahari country of Botswana. The other people of the south-west, the yellowish-skinned Hottentots, were one step ahead in having cattle of their own and they showed themselves more adaptable.

One curious piece of evidence suggests that Bushmen and Hottentots were formerly much more widely spread. Certain unusual sounds known as 'clicks' are peculiar among Bantu languages to the south-eastern tribes, the Zulu of Natal and the leading Cape tribe called (if I get the X-sound right!) the Ama Xosa. Now Bushmen and Hottentots also speak clicking languages and it is virtually certain that the southern Bantu acquired these clicks from Hottentots and Bushmen whom they subdued and absorbed but by no means exterminated.

As early as 1510 the Portuguese visited Table Bay, but it was only in 1652 that the Dutch East India Company decided that their ships must have a port of call and Table Bay was the obvious choice. As I have said, the south-west is generally arid, but there is one important exception. About Cape Town, and only there, the coast juts out into the Atlantic sufficiently to catch the north-west wind straight off the sea. A knot of mountains helps precipitation and this one small corner gets regular winter rain and enjoys, in truth, a perfect Mediterranean climate. A colony was the last thing the East India Company thought of: they wanted only meat and fresh vegetables for passing ships' crews: but the Hottentots grew nothing and their supply of cattle was unreliable. A few burghers, or colonists, were therefore brought in to grow food and rear cattle. About 1688 these got the important reinforcement of about two hundred better-equipped French Huguenot refugees; and because the Hottentots, besides being few and elusive, were very poor workers almost from the beginning, slaves began to be brought in. Among these, Malays from the East Indies were at once a most useful and a colourful enrichment of the working population of Cape Town.

When in spite of the Company's opposition, the colony slowly grew, the fate of the Hottentots was peculiar. There were none of the usual 'native wars' with them. The name of the mountains just beyond Cape Town reminds us that at first the neighbouring district was recognized as the '*Hottentot's Holland*'; but these people were given no legal rights or status, and the new conditions brought smallpox and probably, also milder 'new' infections against which, in those pre-medical days, they had no resistance. Many died. But in early days there was even a little intermarriage and for a long time a good deal of casual 'miscegenation'. A few of the mixed people even kept their own cattle, the frontier group of Griquas, for example, who were impolitely termed 'Bastards'. The pressure that grew, on the one hand requiring Hottentots to give their labour, on the other to secure their legal protection, belongs to the later story of the colonial frontier. After the Act of 1833, by which the British Government abolished slavery throughout their territories, both slaves and 'Hottentots' (still often so called) were free: yet a letter of 1838 I once read was probably right in saying that no one in those days had ever seen a 'pure' Hottentot. Freed slaves and free Hottentots, moreover, became indistinguishable. The Malays, indeed, who provided most of the skilled tradesmen there were, retained some individuality; their mosques, the men's red fezzes, the women's vivid saris, are a feature of Cape Town. Even the Afrikaner people acquired from the Malays some songs and dances, several characteristic Afrikaans words (like the familiar *baaie*, meaning *much*, or *very*) and quite a few of their favourite oriental dishes. Thus the original Hottentots, their blood mixed with that of Europeans, Africans, Malays, are the stock from which there sprang that Afrikaans-speaking, united, wholly westernized people, who are still 50 per cent. of the population of the western and the older districts of South Africa—the Cape Coloured People.

The struggle which originally won this people's freedom, is central to the history of the wider South Africa. Just because this Company so little wanted a colony on its hands, its own restrictive regulations, and the mere lure of the veld, drew the colonists outwards. Here, once again, the rainfall largely decided the outcome. The road to the north was impossible: in that direction land actually to be seen from the top of Table Mountain, if not from Cape Town itself, gets an annual rainfall of only ten inches or less. The only way forward was eastwards along the coastal belt. The going was slow and heavy for even there the rainfall became increasingly uncertain till the advancing Boers reached the region of the south-east summer rains—and then the African tribes the

'Kaffirs', so-called, were there before them. By the time the races first clashed, only in the 1770s, the admirably free and robustly individualist frontier Boers had become a highly distinctive people in their own right. But they were unfortunately isolated; they knew nothing of the Enlightment of the eighteenth century, just as later, their outlook was untouched by the mellowing influence of nineteenth century liberalism. It was actually the Bushmen who taught them to organize their own defence: these Bushmen, who knew nothing of treaties, looked on the water-holes the farmers wanted for their cattle as theirs; these were their most reliable hunting ground. It even came to something like 'war'. The Company could not, if it would, have policed the vast interior and it left the Boers to manage for themselves. The voluntary levies known as *commandos* became their instrument. Left to themselves they would fain have dominated 'Kaffirland' in the same way.

The 'Kaffirs', however, were more formidable and the Government stepped in. The year 1778 saw the first (but not the last) venture in 'segregation'. The Fish River was to separate the rivals; but it was an ambiguous and unsatisfactory boundary and a long series of 'Kaffir' wars followed. The colony was actually held on this Fish River line, virtually till 1848, and the frontier became explosive. Though the Company government was both slack and weak as an upholder of law, individuals did their best: one Company official, Maynier by name, incurred the odium of farmers by what they regarded as his sentimental regard for the rights of 'savages' and even of Hottentots. When these rightless servants had grievances against their farmer-masters, many fled to join the more formidable enemy and make common cause with the 'Kaffirs', so that by the end of the eighteenth century even Hottentot rights had to be considered. At the same point new factors came into play: in 1798 the London Missionary Society began work on the frontier, providing both Hottentots and Kaffirs with the first of a line of stalwart champions, and finally in 1806, the Cape came under British rule. Not long afterwards the British anti-slavery movement was gathering head and its leaders, Wilberforce and Buxton, readily took up the cause also of the 'free people of colour' or Hottentots.

It was an unfortunate chance that the British 'take over' of the Cape and the missionary and anti-slavery movements exactly synchronized. The last Dutch governor, General Janssens, laid it down that none must be suffered to do these people a wrong. The first of the permanent line of British Governors enacted the first (not markedly liberal) Hottentot Code of Laws on lines first drafted by his Dutch predecessor. Thereupon the more recalcitrant Boers, successors of those who had already repudiated the likes of Maynier and Janssens, turned sharply against the new British and allegedly missionary dominated rulers. The Cape Coloured successors of the Hottentots fitted in reasonably well—had they been all. But a Boer versus British feud arose and persisted, utterly preventing any stable *modus vivendi* with the tougher and far more numerous African tribesmen whom strong bands of emigrant Boers found in possession, and extruded, in the course of their steady nineteenth century expansion into the allegedly 'empty' north.

CHAPTER FOURTEEN

The African Achievement

Roland Oliver

THE TOUR of pre-colonial Africa is now complete. It could, of course, have been accomplished in more detail, but more detail would not necessarily have left a clearer picture. For, as we have seen, most of the evidence which bears on African history is indirect evidence. There are no state papers, and few chronicles. The picture is built up partly from stones and bones and hardware, the less perishable parts of man's material equipment; partly by a process of arguing backwards from the situation we know today, in such things as the relationship of languages to one another, or the close similarity of customs and culture; partly from the known history of the countries on Africa's literate northern and eastern fringes; partly from what illiterate peoples have handed down about their own past and partly from what visitors from literate societies have written down or reported to others. So far as the bulk of the continent is concerned, we cannot hear the people of the past speaking to us in their own language. We can only walk round the perimeter-wall of African history, peering in wherever there is a window. As we get to know the perimeter better, we keep on finding more windows. But we can never hope to go right in.

What, then, is the total picture that builds up as we peer through the glass, itself so often stained or frosted? Is it the Africa of unmitigated savagery, complete with cannibalism, witch-doctors, and poisoned darts, which was once so typically pictured by the European imagination? Or is it the ancient Africa of the modern nationalist's dream—rich, learned, colourful, ceremonious, peaceful, free? The answer is certainly neither the one nor the other. The states of the Sudanic belt immediately to the south of the Sahara—ancient Ghana, Mali, Gao, the Hausa states, Bornu, Kanem, Darfur, Sennar, Ethiopia, Adel—all these enjoyed two great advantages over the African lands to the south. In a climate and terrain suited to the horse and the camel, their rulers, soldiers and traders enjoyed a mobility that was unknown elsewhere. They could raid or rule hundreds of miles from their capitals. And they could trade across the deserts, and so keep contact with the general progress of mankind in the Mediterranean and the Middle East. The monsoon winds and the sailing-dhow gave to the merchant cities of the East African coastline the second of these advantages, though not the first. The great difference between the Middle East and medieval Europe was of course the religious difference between Islam and Christianity. Otherwise, in material and intellectual things at least, the world of Islam was ahead of medieval Europe. Certainly Islam's African fringe can bear comparison with Christendom's northern European fringe at any time up to the late sixteenth century. It was in the seventeenth and eighteenth centuries that Europe, and especially northern Europe, drew ahead.

Inland from the East African coast, however, and southward from the Sudanic belt, there began the domain of the forest and the mosquito, the termite and the tse-tse fly, where all movement was on foot or by canoe, all land transport on the human head or shoulder. Not until the very late nineteenth century were even European resources sufficient to overcome these isolating factors. And yet, as we have seen, through all the preceding centuries, the conditions of human life in Africa had not stood still. Virtually the whole continent—the Bushman alone excepted—had passed from the Stone to the Iron Age, from a hard, short life of hunting, fishing, gathering and grubbing, to a relatively settled and prosperous condition of subsistence agriculture and stock-raising. Measured by its material possessions, life was still simple, though simplicity in a tropical climate involved less hardship than in northern latitudes. We may be sure that an easier life was lived in the round houses of Africa than in the cottages of medieval Europe's serfs and free peasants. Certainly the African peasant enjoyed more leisure. Writing of some of the poorer East African peoples in the middle of the nineteenth century, the explorer Burton pronounced them better off in every respect than the Indian peasants he had known before.

It was to the wealth of the minority in town and manor-house that Africa south of the Sudanic belt could offer no parallel to even medieval Europe. The African chief, like the Saxon king or Viking earl, was richer than his subjects mainly in the size of his herds, his granary and his beer-pots, in his power to maintain a great household and to exercise a lavish hospitality. It was above all the impermanence of building materials—the centre-post of a thatched house seldom lasted more than ten years—which precluded attention to decoration and furnishing and the systematic laying up of treasure from one generation to the next which has so much to do with the emergence of individualism in life and art. Nevertheless African courts had their artificers and even their artists. Sculpture in wood and clay from widespread regions of West and West Central Africa has excited the admiration of the outside world, and when crowned with the metal-casting technique of Ife and Benin, achieved the perfection of the very highest art. African oral literature has been much less widely studied, but it is clear from recent translations of the court poetry developed over three centuries in the mountain kingdom of Ruanda, in the very centre of the continent, that literacy is no necessary accompaniment to intelligence, wit, refinement of imagery and delicacy of expression. The unknown architects of Southern Rhodesian chiefs developed over several hundred years a technique of stone-building utilizing and harmonizing with the natural features of the granite outcrops so characteristic of their countryside with an artistry that compels admiration in the most unsympathetic and prejudiced minds.

What is lacking, however, from one end of tropical Africa,

to the other, was the stimulus of long-distance trade and travel, which is as necessary to civilization as the circulation of the blood to the human body. For mankind is one, and the discovery of a single individual is potentially the gain of all the race, providing only that there is communication. Probably not a single one of the millions of individuals who have repeated the racialist cliché that 'the African never even invented the wheel', would himself have had the genius to do so. What such people are asserting is their own good fortune in having been born of ancestors who lived in the main stream of human progress. The geographical environment of most of Africa has been such as to minimize communication with the main stream. It has also been such as drastically to limit the natural growth of population. Though the largest of the continents, all Africa has today a population of some 200 million, half that of India, a third of that of China. It is a fair assumption from known statistics that this population has doubled in the last century, and that of the 100 million of the 1860s, at least a quarter was concentrated in Egypt and North Africa. Save for a few exceptionally well-favoured regions, therefore, the picture is one of serious underpopulation, of small, isolated communities gaining painful mastery over the all-devouring bush.

When this is remembered, the political achievement of many African peoples becomes quite impressive. Not merely in one or two isolated instances, but in large areas scattered over most of the continent, we find the existence of organized states, comparable in population and perhaps in law and order, with the Anglo-Saxon kingdoms of England, occasionally with the England of King Alfred, sometimes even with that of William the Conqueror. These African states, whether in Guinea or the Congo Basin, in Uganda or Rhodesia, seem, like most other states in the world, to have had their origin in immigration and conquest, usually by minorities of invaders who were better armed and organized than those who were there before. It was no doubt in this way that many technical as well as political advances spread southwards into tropical Africa from the Nile valley and the kingdoms of the Sudanic belt. The trend was not always, however, progressive. Time and again in Africa, as in the Dark Ages of Europe and later, we find groups of people who suddenly ceased to be producers themselves, who went over onto a war footing and lived by plunder and loot, often migrating for hundreds and even thousands of miles in the process, like the Vandals and Visigoths of old. Such were the Zimbas who swept up the east coast of Africa in the late sixteenth century, the Jagas who harried the Congo kingdoms in the seventeenth century, and the various Zulu hordes which in the early nineteenth century streamed northwards from Natal incorporating new members from every tribe they encountered en route, and settling finally as the Matabele of Southern Rhodesia, the Shangaans of Southern Mozambique and the Ngoni of Zambia, Malawi, Mozambique and Tanzania. Apart from catastrophic events like these, African states, like all others, had their ups and downs. Confederacies formed and dissolved. Dynasties rose and fell, and, above all, subdivided. It was perhaps the greatest weakness of African monarchies that they never hit upon the principle of primogeniture, nor upon any other certain system of succession. It was in deciding upon a successor to the chieftainship that stability was most severely threatened, and that more powerful states found their best opportunities of intervening in the affairs of their weaker neighbours.

There is no doubt that the effects upon African society of the early contacts with Europe and the outside world in the sixteenth, seventeenth and eighteenth centuries were almost wholly harmful. In agriculture there were great advances, especially from the contact with South America. Maize, manioc, sweet potatoes, peppers, pineapples and tobacco were all introduced into Africa by the Portuguese, and their cultivation spread from tribe to tribe with an amazing rapidity, causing an almost total revolution in food supplies. For the rest, early European influence was strong enough to be profoundly disturbing, yet not strong or direct enough to be constructive. Christian missionary efforts during the first three centuries of European contact lacked the organization, the means of regular communication and supply and, above all, the knowledge of tropical diseases and their remedies, to plant and tend a system of faith and morals that ran counter to many deep-rooted African beliefs and customs. Far stronger during these centuries was the influence of the slave-trader, that most paradoxical product of a Christian society, who without even himself having to master the problems of living in Africa, could, merely by landing his cargoes of guns and drink and hardware, set armies marching and cause the rise and fall of states hundreds of miles distant in the far interior. Right round the western side of Africa from the Senegal to Angola, and for four or five hundred miles inland, the Atlantic trade became the dominant factor in African politics. There were those who gained by it as well as those who lost, but the total effect was certainly corrosive. The rise of the Ashanti Confederacy and the kingdom of Dahomey were offset by the steady decline of the Yoruba civilization and that of Benin, by the disintegration of the Kongo king-dom and the bleeding of Angola. On the east coast the effect of the precarious Portuguese footholds in Mozambique and on the Zambezi was to cut off the Monomatapa's kingdom from its external trade, to hasten the disintegration of its com-ponent parts and finally to turn the Monomatapa into a puppet dependent on the support of Portuguese arms. Farther north, the Portuguese saved the kingdom of Ethiopia at a critical moment in its history and perhaps did something to check the southward expansion of the Turks from the Red Sea. Otherwise their influence was all of a negative kind. They killed the economic life of the east coast, starved Kilwa, oppressed Mombasa. North of the Zambezi they were en-tirely ignorant of the interior. The baneful influence of the early years of European contact was completed by the south-ward spread of European firearms in Moorish hands from Morocco to the western Sudan, from Tripoli to Bornu, from Egypt to Sennar and Darfur.

It was in the nineteenth century that outside influences, becoming stronger and more direct, started to be an asset rather than a liability. This was partly due to a radical development in Western Christendom, which came to see slavery and the slave-trade as social evils which could no longer be tolerated and which set in hand the search for alternative means of contact. But mainly it was due to the revolution in means of production, communication and destruction which carried Europe so far ahead of the rest of the world and so decisively increased its power to intervene in other continents. This revolution released other energies of all kinds, the energies of the trader, the manufacturer, and the miner; the energies of government expressed through consuls and soldiers and administrators; and not least the energies of missionaries and educators. The opening-up and partition of Africa by the European powers during the second half of the nineteenth century is of course the greatest event in African history. Inevitably, it meant a further round of destruction and deterioration in things African, arts and crafts, language and oral literature, social and political institutions, religious beliefs. Not all these things were valuable, and certainly in most cases the gain involved in access to the advances of the outside world, far, far outweighed the domestic loss. In general the things of Europe triumphed, not because they were European, but because they represented the main stream of human progress in what were historically and geographically the most favoured portions of the earth. And, quite certainly, if things European continue triumphant in Africa, it will not be because they are European or operated by Europeans, but because they have been shared with Africans and adopted by Africans as their own.

The pre-colonial history of Africa, therefore, is not of any particular significance either as a weapon in the anti-imperialist struggle or as a pointer to the state of things in some post-colonial, pan-African future. The significance of African history is historical and philosophical. It is the study of man's achievement against a particular inheritance and environment. 'Twenty thousand families', Winston Churchill once wrote of neolithic Britain, 'and all this fine estate, and no work but warfare and hunting.' Through the accumulated experience of those 20,000 and their descendants, and through that of their various conquerors and foreign teachers, the estate now supports 48 million. Whose achievement is the greater? That of the neolithic hunter, laboriously chipping his own arrow-heads and feeding his family by his cunning, his experience, his endurance and his strong right arm? Or that of the modern farmer with his tractor and his combine-harvester, his concrete silo and his electric milking machines? The only answer we can give is that the second could not have existed without the first. It is in the judgement of man's performance in the light of his numbers and of the means at his disposal that the earlier history of Africa, too, has its interest and its value.

Index

Abrehā, Governor, 27

Abyssinia (Habashat), 23

Adal, Muslim kingdom, 47–8

Africa, classical history and, 10, 13, 14–18, 20, 23, 27; circumnavigation, 17; varying mobility in, 97; compared with Europe, 97, 98; population, 99

Africa, East, trade routes, 45–8, 51, 58; medieval towns, 50, 52; coastline, 97

Africa, North, 5, 9, 99; classical history, 13–16; Punic civilization, 17–18; Roman occupation, 18–21; Vandal conquest, 20; Arab invaders, 20, 30, 33; Bedouin invasions, 35–6, 61; Muslim conquest, 61

Africa, southern, 2, 88, 95; peoples of, 88–9, 90–5; geographical influences, 90, 91, 92, 93

Africa, West, 6, 11, 34; maritime exploration, 17; Islam and, 37, 63; events contemporary with English history, 38–43; slave trade, 68, 70, 72

Agriculture, 4, 18–19, 58, 65, 76–7, 80, 84, 85, 86

Akwamu, 70, 73

al-Bakri, on Ghana, 39

Alexandria, 25

Algeria, 15, 31, 36, 42

Ambuila, Battle of, 81

Americas, the, slave trade, 68, 72, 74; crops from, 84, 86, 100

Angola, 75, 83, 84, 87, 91, 101

Ankole, kingdom of, 57–8, 59

Arabia, 30, 31, 33; Bedouin tribes, 35–6; Wahabi movement, 66

Arabs, 27, 31, 37, 61; and N. Africa, 20–1, 30, 31ff.; contact with Negro world, 37–8; and learning, 37–43 *passim;* and E. Africa, 45–7, 51, 55, 58

Ashanti, 68, 101; Golden Stool, 73

Asia, 1, 5, 35, 61

Askia the Great, 41–2

Aswan, tomb inscriptions, 8

Atbara, 26

Assyria, 10, 14

Australopithecus, 2

Axum, 11, 25, 27, 28, 47; Semitic settlement, 22–3, 29; kingly descent, 23; and Meroe, 26–7

Badagri, 72

Banu Hilal and Sulaym, invasion of N. Africa, 35–6

Bechuanaland (Botswana), 88, 91

Benin, 68, 72; craftsmanship, 6, 98; history, 70–1, 101

Berbers, 5, 14–15, 35, 61; Punic influence, 17–18; and Arabs, 31, 33, 34–5; their Empire, 35, 39

Bornu, 61, 63–4, 97, 101; and Fulani *jihad,* 67

Burial customs, 11, 82, 83

Cape Guardafui, 45, 47

Cape Town, 90, 91, 92, 93

Carthage, 13, 15–17; Roman destruction, 17–18; influence of, 18; tombs, 18

China, 30, 48, 53

Christianity, 19, 21, 102; in Ethiopia, 25, 26, 28, 29; in the Yemen, 26; in the Congo, 77–8, 79–81 *passim;* and Islam, 97

Congo (Kongo), 58, 75–7, 87; failure to Westernize, 79–80; decline, 81

Congo river, 75, 82

Copper workings, 82, 84, 85

Cush, 9–10, 11, 26

Cyrenaica, 15, 16, 19, 20

Dahomey, 68, 72, 73, 101

Darfur, 97, 101

Dom Affonso I, 77, 78, 79, 80

Dom Henrique, Bishop of Utica, 77–8

Dunama Dibbalemi, 63

Dutch East India Company, 92, 93–4

Egypt, 30, 42, 99, 101; civilization, 1, 4, 7, 14; the Hamites, 5, 14, 22, 28; and Cush, 9–10; and Axum, 23; Arab conquest, 35

El Kanemi, 67

England, 4, 48, 93; compared with Africa, 99

Ethiopia, 58, 97, 101; origins, 22–3; Solomonic descent, 23, 28; early Church, 23, 25, 28; cultural influences, 27; Zāguē dynasty, 28

Europe and Europeans, 35, 48, 97; slave trade, 68, 70, 71; and Africa, 1, 4–5, 70–4, 84, 87, 88–9, 91–5, 100–2
Ēzanā, King of Axum, 25, 26–7

Fatimids, N. African Empire, 35, 36
Firearms, 63, 72, 73–4, 80, 84, 101
Fish River, 94
France, 31; Grimaldi skulls, 5

Gades, 15
Gao, 38, 41–2, 43, 97
Ghana, 35, 38–9, 68; decline, 40, 43
Gobir, 64, 66
Gold Coast, 38, 72, 73
Gold trade, 11, 16–17, 34, 37 Rhodesian, 47, 48, 55
Guinea, slave trade, 68, 70, 73; Negro kingdoms, 68, 70ff.
Gwandu, Emirs of, 67

Hausa States, 40, 42, 64–5; Fulani jihad and, 64, 65
Homo habilis, finding of, 2–3
Hottentot Code of Laws, 95

Ibn Battuta, 40, 52
Ibn Hawkal, 34
Ibn Khaldun, 36
Idris Alooma, 63, 64
Idris III, 63
Ife, 6, 70, 73, 98
India, 3, 4, 30, 45, 48, 53
Indian Ocean, trading activities, 45, 48–53 passim
Iraq, 30, 33, 36
Iron-working, 10–11, 65, 85; Meroe and, 11, 12, 60–1
Islam, spread in Africa, 30–1, 33, 36, 37, 39–40, 43, 48, 51, 52, 61, 65; Turkish conquest, 35; new religious movement, 35, 66; significance of its introduction, 63; Fulani and, 66–7; and Christianity, 97

Kalahari region, 5, 88, 91
Kālēp, King of Axum, 27
Kanem, 61, 63, 97
Kano, 42, 64, 65
Kasai, 84, 87
Katanga, 82, 83, 84, 87
Katsina, 64, 65
Kayrawan, 31, 33, 36
Kenya, 2, 3, 45

Kenyapithecus wickeri, 3
Kilwa, 47, 50, 52, 101
Kuba, 84–7
Kwango, the, 75, 82, 86

Lagos, 72
Lake Chad, 8, 12–13, 60, 61, 63, 66
Lake Kisale, 82, 83
Lake Moero, 83, 84
Lalibala, rock-hewn churches, 28
Leakey, Dr. L.S.B., 2, 3
Leo Africanus, and Gao, 42–3
Libya, 7, 14, 15, 16, 19, 36
Limpopo, the, 88, 90
Lixus, 15
Loanda, 84, 87
Lopes, Duarte, 80
Luanda Island, 75, 81

Magreb (Maghrib), the, 15, 16, 18–19, 31; Muslim states, 34–5
Mai Omar, 63
Malacca, 50
Malaya, 48, 50, 53
Mali, 38, 40–1, 97
Mansa Musa, 40
Mansa Sulayman, 41
Mashonaland, 53, 59
Mbanza Congo, 75, 77, 78, 80
Mecca, 27, 40
Mediterranean Africa, 4, 7, 13, 15–16, 30; Rome and, 17ff.
Meroe, 10, 11, 26–7; iron workings, 10–11, 60–1
Middle East, 13–14, 30, 60, 97
Migrations, 58–9, 60, 90, 100
Missionaries, Muslim, 33, 34; Christian, 70, 77, 78, 79, 81, 82, 94–5, ·101
Mombasa, 50, 101
Monomatapa, ruler of Zimbabwe, 55–8, 101
Morocco, 15, 31, 34–6, 43, 101
Mozambique, 50, 84, 101

Nakaru, iron-age settlement, 47
Napata, 10
Natal, 89, 90, 91
Negroes, 1, 5–6, 9, 35, 88; in Sudan states, 37–43; and Guinea kingdoms, 68ff.; and the priesthood, 77–8
Niani, 40–1
Nigeria, 6, 9, 61; ethnic characteristics, 60; rise of Northern state, 67

Nile and Nile Valley, 4, 7, 8, 9, 10, 12, 61
Numidia, 18, 19

Obalokun, King, 71
Okomfo Anokye, 73
Old Stone Age, 4, 5
Olduvai, 'Nutcracker Man', 2; *Homo habilis*, 2-3
Olorgesaile, hand-axes, 3-4
Osei Tutu, King, 73
Oyo Empire, 68, 70-3

Pakistan, Siwaliks discovery, 3
Pate, 51
Pemba Island, 51
Pereira, Pacheco, and Benin, 70
Periplus of the Erythraean Sea, 22, 23, 47
Persia, 13, 14, 30, 33, 52
Phoenicia, 15-17, 53
Port Durnford, 47
Portugal, and Africa, 70, 75-82 *passim*, 84, 88, 91, 100, 101

Qadriga order, 66

Races and tribes: Aja, 72; Almohads, 36; Almoravids, 34, 36, 39, 40; Amaxosa, 91; Austuriani, 20; Bantu, 5, 75-7, 80-1, 88-9, 90; Basuto, 90; Bavenda, 90; Bororoje, 66; Bulala, 63; Bushmen, 5, 91-2, 94, 97; Bushong, 85, 86, 87; Cape Coloured, 93, 95; Chokwe, 84, 87; Edo, 68; Fulani, 65-7; Gaetuli, 19; Garamantes, 19; Griquas, 93; Hausa, 64-5; Herero, 90; Hottentots, 5, 91-5; Jagas, 79, 80, 85, 100; 'Kaffirs', 88, 90, 93; Kuba, 85-7; Leuathae, 20; Luba, 83, 84, 87; Lunda, 83, 84, 86, 87; Makaranga, 55-6; Mandingo, 40; Mashona, 55; Matabele, 100; Mazices, 20; Ngoni, 100; Ovimbundu, 83, 84, 87; Pygmies, 5; Sarakole, 38; Shangaans, 100; Songhai, 41-2; Songye, 83, 87; Sosso, 40; Tswana, 90; Yorubas, 68, 70, 101; Zimbas, 100; Ziwa, 47; Zulus, 90, 91, 100
Rano, 64, 65
Rhodesia, 47, 88; Zimbabwe ruins, 53ff., 98
Rock paintings, 9, 91
Rome, and N. Africa, 13, 16-21; and Malaya, 48

Rotse kingdom, 83
Ruanda, 57, 58, 59, 98

Sahara, the, 5, 7, 13, 30, 37, 40, 42; Roman occupation, 19-21; caravan routes, 61, 65
St Takla Haymanot, 28
Senegal, the, 38, 40, 66, 101
Sennar, 97, 101
Shaka, 90
Shyaam a Mbul a Ngoong, 86
Sicily, 16, 31, 35
Slave trade, 34, 37, 46, 47, 48, 64, 65, 92, 95, 102; Atlantic, 68, 70-4 *passim*, 101; effect of, 101
Sokoto, Emirs of, 67
Somalia, 2, 45, 52
Songhai, 64, 65
Songo Mnara, 50
Spain, 15, 16, 31, 35
Sudan, Central, 61, 63, 65, 66, 97
Sudan, Western, 7, 10, 11, 26-7, 37; Negro states, 37-43; Islam and, 39-40
Syria, 30, 33, 35, 36

Tanzania, 2-3, 58, 84
Tanganyika, 48
Timbuktu, 40, 43, 77
Tools, 2-3, 10-11
Trade, 8, 9, 15-17, 20, 22, 33-4, 35, 37, 45-52 *passim*, 70, 73-4, 77, 83-4
Transvaal, 2, 89
Tripoli, 20, 42, 63, 64, 101
Tunis, 15, 31, 34-6, 42, 65
Turkey, 35, 101

Uganda, 57, 58; Miocene fossils, 3
'Uqba ibn Nafi', general, 31
Usuman dan Fodio, revivalist, 66
Utica, 15, 17, 77-8

Vandals, 20

Wadi Halfa, 8, 9
Weapons, 3-4, 9, 10-11
Whydah, 72, 73

Yemen, the, 22, 27, 60
Yorubaland, 71-2

Zambesi, the, 47, 101
Zambia, 83
Zanzibar, 45
Zegzeg (Zaria), 64, 65
Zelia, 48
Zimbabwe stone ruins, 53-8